Out Of Apples?

Understanding Personal Relationships

Lee Schnebly

Publishers: Bill Fisher
Howard Fisher
Helen Fisher
Tom Monroe, P.E.
Coordinator: Veronica Durie
Editor: Judith Schuler
Art Director: Josh Young

Cover Illustration: David Fischer

Published by Fisher Books
P.O. Box 38040
Tucson, AZ 85740-8040
(602) 325-5263

**Library of Congress
Cataloging-in-Publication Data**
Schnebly, Lee M., 1932–
Out of apples?
Bibliography: p.
Includes index.
 1. Self-help techniques.
 2. Life skills,
I. Title

BF632.S37 1987 158'.1 87-19660
ISBN 1-55561-005-6

©1984, 1988, Lee Schnebly

Printed in U.S.A.
Printing 10 9 8 7 6

Fisher Books are available at special quantity discounts for educational use. Special books, or book excerpts, can also be created to fit specific needs. For details please write or telephone.

Contents

I would like to thank Laurie Schnebly, Cynthia Griffis, Al Gyuro and Lisa Schnebly who helped me with this book.

To Bill McCartin,
who taught me about apples and love,
and to Larry,
who gives me both.

I Was "Out of Apples!"

"You have to think of yourself as an apple barrel," he said. "And as an apple barrel, you're worthwhile only if you have some apples."

I listened, nodded, sniffed and continued to cry as he proceeded.

"If you give apples to your children, your husband, your neighbors, your parents, your friends, the church, the PTA . . . why, pretty soon you're out of apples. You're no good to anyone, not even yourself. As an apple barrel, you're unable to function until you get some more apples."

I nodded shakily and blew my nose while he continued.

"For you, getting apples might be going shopping, reading a book or playing the piano. Maybe sewing a new dress or going to lunch with a friend will give you apples or perhaps just being all by yourself for a few hours. You've got to do whatever's important to you because that's how you get apples."

He could see how empty, discouraged and defeated I was. He was showing me the light at the end of the tunnel. I *was* out of apples, and I had never realized it. Nor had I known I was *entitled* to apples. I needed them.

I was in my early 30s and going through a period of depression. I didn't understand why, but I couldn't stop crying. I was physically and emotionally exhausted. I dreaded every day and felt totally defeated by life. My husband, Larry, who is an incredibly sensitive person, didn't think there was a problem. Only *I* thought there was, but I couldn't figure out what it was.

On the surface, I had everything a woman could want—a lovely home, two cars, four beautiful, healthy children, my parents, friends, talents, skills. My neighbor had advised me just the day before, "Snap out of it, Lee. Look at all you have to be thankful for. Why should you be depressed?"

And I had thought, "Yeah, I guess I do have everything. I've got to stop feeling depressed. It's not fair to my family."

I'd been crying more and more during those days. I hurried to my bedroom when I felt the tears coming because I didn't want to upset the kids. Sometimes they'd see me crying anyway, then I'd feel guilty for being depressed and try harder to be cheerful. Sometimes they'd ask me what was wrong, with genuine concern. I would say I was just tired. And I'd sit with them on the couch and read them a story, to make it up to them that I'd been a cause of concern. The last thing I wanted was to see them unhappy.

Fortunately for all of us, I was in good hands. I began some intensive counseling with Bill McCartin, a priest who was to become my mentor and educator and one of my dearest friends. I began to understand some of my mistaken beliefs. As I realized how unnecessary they were, I started changing them to more-productive ones.

With counseling from Bill and with love and support from my family, I read everything I could get my hands on about mental health. The road back was a lot faster and more fun than the road down had been. In a relatively short time, I was enjoying life again. Eventually I returned to school for my master's degree in counseling and guidance. I'm now in private practice as a counselor.

In this book I want to share some of the insights and values that have helped me become a happier person and enabled me to help others to do the same.

Occasionally I announce to the family, "I am out of apples." They all scoot away to their various pursuits, knowing I have nothing left to give them. Then I set about getting more apples.

Writing this book gives me a lot. I hope reading it will give some apples to you!

Understanding Self-Esteem

Let's look at mental health on a scale of 1 to 100. At the bottom, number 1, is the person who is totally maladjusted and unable to cope with life at all. He's probably confined to a mental hospital or cared for entirely by others. At the top, number 100, is the person who is the picture of self-reliance and confidence. He's completely able to handle *anything* life gives him. He feels comfortably confident all the time. He's happy knowing nothing that comes his way will be insurmountable. He knows he can solve any problem or leap any hurdle. He meets life head on, eager to see what's next, happy with almost everyone he meets because he's happy with himself.

If 100 is the epitome of mental health, I guess we're all mentally ill to some degree. I don't believe we'll *ever* make that 100 mark because perfection just isn't possible.

But wherever we are on the mental-health scale, we can rate ourselves at exactly the same number for self-esteem. The two go hand in hand. In fact, every psychological problem we have is directly proportionate to a deficiency in our self-esteem.

If I ever reached 100 on the scale of mental health and self-esteem, I'd have no more psychological problems at all. I'd have other problems, such as flat tires, budgets, colds and weeds. But there'd be no more psychological problems, such as anxiety, fear, jealousy, doubt, insecurity and inferiority feelings. With problems like those out of the way, I could deal with flat tires and budgets any day. They're easy to deal with compared to emotional difficulties.

How did our self-esteem get so low in the first place? Alfred Adler, one of the fathers of psychiatry, said man was born feeling inferior, and he spends his life trying to increase his feelings of mastery, superiority and significance.

That wouldn't be so hard to do *if* we all got unconditional love as children. But we don't. As babies, we begin looking around us, watching life happen. We watch our parents, siblings and grandparents. We lie there in our little cribs and observe. We move into our playpens and observe. We cry and observe, smile and observe, get angry and observe, obey or disobey and observe. With every action we observe the reactions of those around us.

"Children are excellent observers," said Adler, "and poor interpreters." He was an optometrist before he became a psychiatrist, so he compared the observation process with creating a pair of glasses. He said as tiny tots we observe and grind our lenses. We keep watching and deciding how life works. We grind lenses until we finish our particular eyeglass prescription at about age 5. Then we polish our eyeglasses, put them on and look through them for the rest of our lives. Those glasses are the viewpoint through which we look at life.

Sometimes we discover at age 40 we're still wearing the same glasses we created at age 5. We're long overdue for a prescription change. It's fortunate we're free to change lenses anytime we want. It's great fun to begin seeing life through new ones!

We make thousands of decisions in the process of grinding our lenses during those early years. Those decisions are judgments of what life is all about and how we can best fit into it. We live with our beliefs for years and years, maybe forever.

But a lot of our beliefs are *mistaken beliefs*. They seem sound to us as children, and sometimes we cling to them even as adults. But if we look hard at them, frequently we choose to throw them out.

One belief might be we are worthwhile only if we are pleasing others, especially those people who are important to us.

We assume when Mom glares at us, yells at us or spanks us, we must be bad. We don't realize she is trying to teach us right from wrong or she is tired and grouchy. Our assumption is, "Uh-oh. I'm bad and rotten. Mom doesn't love me anymore. I'll have to try harder not to spill juice or make any mistakes because I can't stand it when she's mad at me!" Our self-esteem just dropped a few points.

It drops a lot when we're babies, but it also rises a great deal as we discover how many points we can make by smiling, learning to talk and walk, eating with a spoon and so on. Closely, carefully, we watch Mom's face to see if we're good or bad. We go up 2 points and down 1, up 5 and down 3, up 4 and down 8. We're always measuring and watching, then deciding how worthwhile we are.

If Mom loves us only when we're perfect, we receive conditional love. But *unconditional love* goes a long way toward building up the self-esteem we want so badly. But most of us never received it. We all measured ourselves and came up short. And we all share inferiority complexes.

But don't worry . . . it can actually be fun building up our self-esteem once we give ourselves permission to do it! How do we begin building up our self-esteem? First, we need to look back and see how we got attention when we were little.

I Was a Kewpie Doll

I was born in the "Kewpie-doll" era. The Kewpie doll had round, pink cheeks and a big, straight-lined smile. I probably looked like one when I was small because my father immediately dubbed me his "little Kewpie doll." It wasn't hard for me to see I got a lot of attention when I was a Kewpie doll. Life wasn't so good when I wasn't cute and smiling. Before I was 3 years old, I had that Kewpie-doll smile down pat. I smiled my way through the toddler years, grade school, high school and college.

It worked pretty well. I was admired for my nice smile. Life went smoothly as long as I looked and acted like a Kewpie. Kewpie dolls never cried or got angry or did anything unpleasant. What they do, eventually, is *break* . . . which is why I was so depressed when I first sought counseling. I ground that Kewpie-doll smile into my glasses and wore them daily for over 30 years. Till the day he died, my father called me his "little Kewp!"

Why did I cling to that smile for so long? Because it worked! It was my claim to fame. It got me admiration, made me special, made me welcomed at friends' parties and guaranteed a sort of approval everywhere. The unspoken contract between me and the world was, "I won't get mad at you, and you won't get mad at me, OK? I'll smile and so will you, OK?"

If that unspoken contract had always worked, it might have been a perfect device to use for the rest of my life. But it didn't work too much of the time. And even when it did, it caused problems with my self-esteem. If I smiled brightly at a party and people responded to me, approved of me and enjoyed me, I knew I had to continue my Kewpie personality. Obviously that's what they were attracted to. I dared not frown or be grim or say negative things. In other words, I dared not be honest because they might reject me. I couldn't stand that.

So I became an expert at judging people's expressions. I could read on their faces exactly what behavior they liked from me. I was determined to deliver it to them! I agreed with their political beliefs, their religious philosophies, whatever it was they had to say. Disagree? Never! There was too much at stake. It was much easier to play the game, to please, to pretend, to sharpen my skills at measuring up to their expectations. I reveled in their approval of me. It was too dangerous to risk rejection by asserting myself.

I loved hearing people say how "nice" I was. But inside

I cringed. I could only think someday I might fail to measure up. Then they would be finished with me forever. I couldn't stand that.

It was usually easy to be a Kewpie with strangers. I could have them in the palm of my hand in no time, so accomplished was I at charming and pleasing. But after I knew them a little better, it got harder. Getting *on* the pedestal was a piece of cake, but I was forever worrying about falling *off*. What if they saw the real me and didn't like me? What if they discovered I wasn't really happy and optimistic all the time? What if Little Miss Sunshine dared to cry or pout or say a bad word? Unthinkable!

So inside I suffered with the belief I wasn't very good. I just had the world fooled. If they ever got a glimpse of the real me, I thought, they would probably hate me. What a tightrope I walked, trying to be all things to all people. And what a lot of apples I gave away in my efforts to please. Room mother? Sure! Bake a cake for the carnival? Of course! Read me a story? Choose your book.

Having guests for dinner was a challenge I tackled with some regularity because it helped prove what a super person I was. I began early by fixing the food and storing it in the freezer. I assured guests I'd "keep it simple," so if there were a flaw, God forbid, they might excuse it and chalk it up to my devil-may-care attitude. What a laugh!

I began cleaning house the week before, polishing, washing windows, afraid someone would happen upon a dusty corner and be shocked. The day of the party I was a complete wreck, thawing the food, setting a table right out of a magazine, washing the kids, the dog and the main bathroom. I always tried to get the family to use the other bathroom so the guest bath would be immaculate. Usually someone forgot and defaced my sparkling basin with toothpaste just before arrival time.

I was tense, fatigued and churning with anxiety by the time the doorbell rang. But you can be sure no one ever saw it. I glided to the door with a casual air, seemingly a paragon of warmth and confidence. I chatted easily over drinks, after which I served perfect food on my perfect table.

Most people never guessed how fragmented I was. I was aware of my children needing me and felt torn between ministering to their wants and continuing to charm my guests. I was torn between wanting to clean up the kitchen to avoid facing it in the morning and wanting to sit and look contented with the company because that's what I thought they'd like. In the end, waving goodbye to them, I glowed with pleasure at all the compliments I'd received. I knew once again I'd fooled them into thinking I was perfect and relaxed at the same time. But would I be able to measure up again next time? I couldn't stand it if I didn't.

Interestingly, as hard as I worked at it, I was never able to please everyone. I heard remarks from well-meaning friends who quoted someone as having described me as "too goody-goody," "unreal" or "phony." Those descriptions gave me sweaty palms and skyrocketing fears, hinting at my not measuring up to someone's standards. I gave those comments a lot of thought and worry, processing the information and trying to decide how to handle it. It was as if with more effort I would surely be able to measure up to *everyone's* expectations.

One neighbor even hinted I must be neurotic. I have her to thank for helping me discover the first book I ever read on mental health. I was in a drugstore one day and saw a book titled *Be Glad You're Neurotic,* by Louis E. Bisch. Casting furtive glances around me to make sure no one noticed, I took it gingerly and glanced at the index page. I was astonished. Even from that sketchy description, it seemed the book had been written about *me.*

I bought it, rushed home and read it that day. It was a real breakthrough for me. Now I *knew* I was neurotic, but the author almost convinced me I was OK in spite of it. Could it be I was worthwhile after all? I was entering a new phase in my life.

The chief value of that delightful book was the concept that most of us are neurotic to some degree, but we are nifty people nonetheless. That was probably the first time I had an inkling it was all right *not* to be perfect. I found that concept encouraging and reassuring. I still recommend the book to friends and clients.

I personally stumbled onto the Kewpie-doll mask, but there are hundreds of others from which people can choose. For instance, the mask of a comedian. You may know some. Not professional comedians, just ordinary folks like you and me. They always have a joke for every situation. A laugh a minute, hilarious—they're the life of the party. But you never really get to know them because they're afraid you might not like them.

I have other friends with perpetual chips on their shoulders. A grim remark, a frown and a hostile attitude keep them apart from people. They're safe from real intimacy. Inside those people are the same feelings of doubt and inadequacy that plague Kewpies, jokers and everyone else.

We don't need masks, but we always thought we did.

We picked up that theory in our toddler days when we were busily grinding those glasses full of mistaken beliefs. We never suspected any mistakes. We adopted the belief hook, line and sinker. All of us bought different ones, but whichever beliefs we chose, we clung to them for our very lives. We would have defended them hotly had anyone challenged them.

Challenging Our Beliefs

Now that we're grown up, we can challenge our own lifelong beliefs. When we examine our beliefs with logic, we'll probably choose to keep about 90% of them. It's the other 10% that really complicates our lives.

Let's look at some beliefs that seem to be present in many of us. One is *I need to please people. I must have their approval at all times.*

First we must differentiate between "need" and "want." I suppose it would be lovely to have everyone's approval all the time, but that would be only a "want" rather than a "need." I might *want* a hot-fudge sundae every day, but no way can I convince myself or my bathroom scales I *need* one. And it would be nice to have people approve of me at all times, but I know it's totally impossible.

If I cut my hair short to please my mother, I might offend my aunt who loves long hair. If I fix baked potatoes for one son, I offend the other who loves french fries. There's no way I can win the game of pleasing everyone, so logically I must make the decision to quit trying.

But I may protest at the idea. What if someone gets mad at me? I can't stand that!

"I can't stand that" is a saying many of us use frequently, without much thought. Dr. Albert Ellis, a noted psychologist and author, maintains there is nothing we *can't* stand. We just think we can't stand things.

At a workshop Dr. Ellis gave in Tucson, he suggested we change our terminology to something more mild, such as "I would be uncomfortable if . . . " but never again use the words "I can't stand . . . " He frequently asks his clients to deliberately put themselves in uncomfortable or unpleasant positions then endure it, proving to themselves they can stand it very well.

Dr. Ellis lives in New York City. He recommends a client take a subway ride and call out the streets loudly to the whole car. "Forty-Second Street!" As the heads turn toward him with surprise, disapproval, annoyance, fascination, amusement or whatever, the caller continues to call out streets and assures himself silently he *can* stand it. As he continues to stand it, he begins to feel a kind of excitement and an awareness of a strength he may never have known he had.

Ellis told our group if there are no subways in town to go to a department store, stand near the escalator and call out the time. A lusty "10:38!" should make heads turn. We could continue the process until asked to leave or until we're sufficiently certain we can stand it. What a heady feeling it would be as we left the store—even if we're being escorted out by management. We'd know deep down for perhaps the first time we can tolerate disapproval as well as anyone.

I must admit I haven't deliberately put myself into a situation as Ellis suggests. But when I find myself in some uncomfortable spot, I realize I have another opportunity to prove to myself I *can* stand disapproval. I can even grow stronger with it.

I live off a very busy street that has long lines of traffic going in both directions during rush hour. I used to sit tensely at the wheel, head swinging anxiously from side to side. I'd wait for a safe break in the traffic to make my left turn. Aware of cars beginning to stack up behind me, I squirmed in agony. I was sure they were cursing me and saying things like, "There's a woman driver for you, Martha. She's missed three chances to get out there. Look, she could have gone then. Maybe if I honk . . . " And at the sound of the honks, I felt ashamed, embarrassed and ready to skip out in the line of traffic whether or not it was safe, just to avoid further hostility or rejection.

After hearing Ellis, I now sit calmly at the wheel, confident I'll know when the time is right to turn. Meanwhile, I have a chance to prove to myself once again I can stand disapproval! That negative situation has become a positive one simply by my changing my belief from "I can't stand it" to "I *can* stand it!"

With that exercise, I've also managed to prove to myself I don't need other people's approval. I don't have to please people after all. I can tolerate their hostility, their disapproval and their total rejection if that's the case. I can become stronger for it!

I can also change my fantasy about what people behind me are thinking. Possibly the man was saying, "Martha, that little lady up ahead is a good driver, you know that? Some people would have tried a left turn then but not her. She knows how to judge distance, and she's not moving till the time is right. I think I'll honk a good morning to her, yesiree." Because we can't know what they're saying anyway, why not imagine compliments? It's good for our self-esteem.

Another mistaken belief many of us share is *I must be perfect. If I'm not, I'm not worthwhile and I must continue striving to be perfect.*

I can shut my eyes and see Mrs. Johnson in the sixth grade saying, "High ideals, boys and girls. Let's think high ideals. Try harder! Don't give up. Keep trying to improve! If a thing is worth doing, it's worth doing well. Try to get 100 on today's spelling test!"

Well, Mrs. Johnson, I know you meant well, but I have to tell you I disagree. You and the thousands of other well-meaning people who touched our lives did a good job of making us feel rotten about ourselves when we missed five on our tests. B's were not good; C's were dreadful; D's were despicable. We won't even discuss the humiliation of failing. Our self-esteem depended greatly on the kind of grades we got in school. We got the impression we were only as good as our grades.

It's taken me years to learn if a thing is worth doing, it's worth doing *imperfectly.* I can be quite satisfied with myself if I make a mediocre apple pie. It doesn't have to be perfect. If I buy a frozen one and bake it for dessert, I'm every bit as worthwhile as if I'd picked the apples, peeled them, cored them, sliced them, spent a half-hour making pie crust and created a pie that would win a blue ribbon at the fair. If I choose to go to all that trouble, that's fine. But I'm not a better person for having gone through all those motions.

We've learned to judge our worthiness by our accomplishments. Accomplishing tasks and achieving things *can* improve our self-esteem because it's satisfying to create and do things. But in no way do I have to do them perfectly.

Each time I speak on this concept, someone counters with, "But what if I'm a brain surgeon? Don't I have to do a perfect job tying together all those little nerves or whatever brain surgeons do?"

I'm willing to make a concession in that area, especially if you're operating on my brain, Doctor. But for that situation only. When you've sewn your last perfect stitch and taped on your last perfectly wrapped bandage, go out and shoot an imperfect game of golf. Mow your lawn imperfectly. Bake your family some brownies, even if they're soggy and cut into imperfect squares. Read a science-fiction paperback. Give yourself permission to stop striving to be perfect.

It's All Right to Be Imperfect

Give yourself permission to make mistakes. Have the courage to be *imperfect*. What a relief it is to stop trying to measure up to the expectations of others and the even-more-demanding expectations of ourselves!

I remember my neighbor Ruthie. When my children were small, I ran to Ruthie's house occasionally to borrow a can of soup or something. Ruthie came to the door wearing a cute gingham jumpsuit. Her hair was perfect, her three children impeccable and her house immaculate. Ruthie put mandarin oranges and strawberries into cute little gelatin molds. In those days, I was proud of myself if I managed to make a bowl of plain red gelatin once in awhile.

It was painful to compare my ineptness at housekeeping with Ruthie's perfection. I consoled myself with the knowledge I had one more child than she did, until she had a fourth, then a fifth. *Still* her house was perfect. It boggled my mind.

One day, however, Ruthie confided she had an ulcer. I was thrilled beyond words! I wasn't unsympathetic with her discomfort, but it was reassuring to know even Ruthie couldn't be perfect without paying a high price for it. Interestingly, I liked her better after that. She seemed more like "one of us" than some paragon of virtue who defied human understanding.

We don't *need* to be perfect! We can do an OK job of housekeeping or parenting or working outside the house, or all three, and still be worthwhile. I have a sign over my kitchen sink that I hope will be an inspiration to my children. It reads, "Have the courage to be imperfect."

It does take courage to be imperfect. I have to force myself not to clean the top of the refrigerator when we're expecting dinner guests. It's a symbol to me of my willingness to accept myself as I am—not perfect but OK just the same.

I also discovered when I lower my standards for myself, I accept other people more easily and completely. When I held unreasonably high standards for myself, I had the same standards for everyone else. Nobody ever measured up entirely. I always felt disappointed or disillusioned by somebody's behavior. I reasoned if I should try to be perfect, so should they. It's a relief to know I don't have to be perfect, and neither does anyone else.

The value of humility is another mistaken belief. *I mustn't think too well of myself or sound conceited.*

As a child, I learned the art of not accepting compliments by watching two experts, my parents. They always looked humble, and I outdid them in my emulation. If I got a compliment on a dress I made, I quickly explained I'd gotten the fabric on sale for 66¢ a yard and there was this flaw in it, and look, the buttonhole was a little crooked. If people complimented me on my variety of skills, I laughed apologetically and said ruefully, "Oh, I'm the jack-of-all-trades, master of none. I don't do anything really *well!*" Heaven forbid I should say a simple, "Thank you!"

I later discovered the connection between my habit of "humility" and a very common priority that many of us share—"moral superiority." This is discussed on page 118.

When my counselor suggested I make a list of all the good things I thought about myself, I accepted the challenge with fear and trepidation. It was like being told to go out and steal after having learned it was wrong! I began writing dubiously.

"Made the bed pretty well today."

"Always have nice clean hair."

"Cooked breakfast for my family."

"Good at making other people feel happy."

I found I could fill the page pretty easily once I got the hang of it. It got to be fun!

When I made my list, it was the only time I ever wrote things down. But it started a habit of complimenting myself that I still use. When I make a left turn onto the busy street, I tell myself, "Good driver! You make good decisions!" Recently I made a left turn that wasn't too wise because I got dangerously close to hitting another car. My first response to myself was, "You dummy!" but I immediately canceled that. "No, you're not a dummy. You're a very good driver. You made a questionable decision that time, but obviously it wasn't too far off because you didn't collide. Next time you'll be more cautious because you *are* a very good driver."

And I believe it. I *am* a good driver. I'm also a good cook, good seamstress, have a green thumb and a million other things. I'm not perfect in any of them, and that's fine. I like me just the way I am.

Relationships With Others

I'm capable of liking you only as much as I like myself. That's another reason for improving my self-esteem. I want to be able to enjoy other people more. The more I accept myself, the more I accept and genuinely appreciate you!

The wise and wonderful man who told me about getting more apples gave me another gem one day. Bill McCartin said, "You can have as good a relationship with someone as you are honest with him." I've tried it, and he's right. It doesn't matter whether or not I'm honest with the clerk at the drugstore because I see her only occasionally, and we don't pretend to be friends. A smile and, "Have a good day." "Thanks, you too," is about the extent of our conversation. Neither of us has time for more of a relationship than that. But with my husband, my children, my parents and my close friends, I *must* be honest.

By honesty, I don't mean the kind of frankness that can be cruel and unnecessary. I mean an honesty given with kindness and love.

Sharing feelings, faults and philosophies with someone helps me feel good about myself because I've risked self-disclosure and have been accepted anyway. I'm disagreed with sometimes. Sometimes I'm disapproved of. But I'm still accepted, valued and affirmed.

As a Kewpie doll, I was seldom honest because it was too risky to face the possibility of rejection. It's always a risk. I risk your displeasure any time I tell you something. But if I have the courage to take that risk, the courage to let you see my imperfections, I usually find I'm as acceptable as I was before I shared myself. In fact, we may have a better, closer relationship.

All of us have secrets we believe are terrible, horrible and completely unacceptable to mankind. In groups we sometimes write down a horrible secret with identical pencils on identical white squares of paper so they can't be identified. We put the papers in a box, draw them out and take turns reading them. It's fascinating to hear them, knowing we're safe from being identified. Frequently we hear the same ones again and again.

"Sometimes I masturbate."

"I had an affair once, after I was married."

"Sometimes I'm so angry I hate my children and wish I didn't have them."

"I'm very attracted to another man."

"I hate sex."

"I've never told my husband I wasn't a virgin when I married him."

"I don't think I love my wife anymore."

We listen, and sometimes we nod with recognition, sympathy or empathy. But the sky doesn't fall! No one faints from shock. The world continues as before. We've learned everyone has "terrible secrets" like we do. How nice it is when we can tell some to our friends or our husband or wife and feel that same uplifting acceptance. What a boost to our self-esteem when someone knows the worst about us and likes us anyway.

I'm not suggesting we tell everyone everything we know. That would be tiresome. But knowing we're free to share everything we think or feel with someone (and not necessarily always the same person) is an exciting thought. Try it.

Examining Our Feelings

Many times I've heard someone say, "You shouldn't feel that way!" I believed it and felt guilty for feeling whatever way I wasn't supposed to feel. I remember how free I felt when I learned feelings are not right or wrong; they just *are*.

Feelings are like teapots or salt-and-pepper shakers. They simply exist. What I might do with a teapot could be wrong. If I pick it up and pour tea on my neighbor's lap, I've done something wrong. On the other hand, if she had just set fire to her skirt with her cigarette, perhaps I'm doing her a big favor by pouring tea on her lap. You can judge me as right or wrong in how I use the teapot, but the teapot itself cannot be judged for its behavior.

It's the same with feelings. Feelings are important and wonderful, but we must not let them control our lives. We can listen to them, enjoy them, be aware of them, hate them. But we must know they're there to serve *us*, rather than the other way around. If I let my feelings control my life, it's like letting a driverless car speed down the mountain. Feelings are the gas that runs the car, but the car needs a driver to keep it under control.

In the old days, I blamed my feelings for my actions. I could lie on my bed in my darkened room and cry. If I didn't get the laundry done I could say, "I couldn't help it. I just felt too awful to do anything today." Of course, I felt guilty for not doing the laundry. But as long as I assured my family I felt guilty, it excused my behavior. As long as you feel guilty, you must be a responsible and worthwhile person. Right? Wrong! Alfred Adler often said, "Either do something bad or feel guilty, but don't do both. It's too much work."

Many of us assume we can't help our feelings. They just "overcome us." We might think to ourselves, "I am only a helpless victim of anger or sadness or anxiety, and I must just put up with them until they go away." We believe a particular happening or situation causes a certain feeling in us. We have no say in its being there. Dr. Albert Ellis devised an ABC system . It can help us look at our feelings with an eye to controlling them.

A = Action
B = Belief
C = Consequential feelings

We often think an action causes a consequence or feeling. For instance, if I saw a thunderstorm approaching, I would feel uneasy.

A = Thunderstorm
C = Uneasiness

But Ellis pointed out the importance of *B* in that formula. My belief about thunderstorms—they're dangerous—determines my feelings about them.

For example, you and I are sitting on a patio, enjoying our iced tea. Suddenly we hear a rumble in the sky. When we look behind us, we see the sky getting black with giant clouds looming overhead, indicating an approaching storm. That's *A*.

Now let's look at *B*. If I was taught storms can be dangerous, especially when there's lightning and thunder, and if I get caught in one I might be struck by lightning and die, I'd feel uneasiness or fear. The consequential feeling—*C*—for me is fear because of my belief—*B*.

On the other hand, if you come from a family that loved the drama of storms, you might see the situation very differently. Remembering your parents standing out on the porch looking at the black sky and lightning flashes with joyous fascination, you might turn your chair eagerly to get a better view while I hurried for the security of the living room. Your *C* would be happy anticipation because of your belief—*B*—thunderstorms are fascinating.

It's the same approaching storm, *A,* but look how differently we feel about it because of our different beliefs!

We all learn many beliefs in our lifetime. Our feelings are directly related to them. We can look at our beliefs any time. If we decide they don't hold up in the face of logic, we can change them. Some of our beliefs probably will never change because they *will* hold up in the face of logic. They serve us well. We have no need to change those beliefs. But we might have a few that complicate our lives. If we see the value of changing them, our feelings become much more comfortable.

Feeling Guilty

One uncomfortable feeling I encounter frequently in young mothers is the guilt they feel when they leave their children with a sitter or in a nursery school. Many nurseries are excellent, such as those provided by churches where I teach parenting classes. They're clean and well-supervised, with nutritious snacks, educational toys and a low teacher-child ratio. My classes last only 2 hours, which is a relatively short time for children to be in a nursery.

In spite of this, when a mother leaves a child, the child may look imploringly at her and even cry. The mother feels guilty. She may have feelings of "meanness" as she looks at her beloved 2-year-old holding out his arms for her to please rescue him from this fate worse than death. If he continues to cry, Mother may decide it isn't worth attending classes after all. She might take the frightened little tot and run for the security of home. If she leaves him at the nursery and comes to class, she may sit and squirm, half-listening to the presentation and half-preoccupied with what the little tyke might be suffering. Her entire being is wracked with guilt.

I always compliment young mothers for their courage to leave their children in nursery schools occasionally, when they know the facilities and staff are acceptable. But I can easily relate to them and their discomfort. I agonized over the same dreadful dilemma when my children were small. I now see how those feelings were a result of my beliefs.

My mother used to say, "A good mother always takes care of her children. A good mother doesn't leave her child with a sitter, certainly not at a nursery school! A good mother wants her children to be happy. If they are unhappy with a stranger, then a mother should stay home with them. A good mother doesn't trust her children to strangers."

My mother never left me with sitters or at nursery schools, so I had further reason to accept her belief. I went into motherhood determined to treat my children with the same care I received. I was the type of mother who snatched up my child and headed for home. My action-belief-consequential feeling system was:

A = Child is nervous about being left with strangers.

B = A good mother doesn't leave her children with strangers.

C = I am guilty at this dastardly thing I've almost done, so I must grab my child and bolt for home!

My friend, Pam, had a different kind of mother. Pam's mother believed children should become independent and self-reliant as soon as possible, for their own good. One way to accomplish this was to let them learn they could get along without Mom for short periods of time. Pam's mother frequently left her with sitters and in nursery schools. Pam survived beautifully. Naturally she believed children learn strength and independence when left with someone other than Mom for short periods of time. Pam increased the length of those times gradually but regularly. Leaving her children was a piece of cake for Pam because of her belief. Let's look at her ABC formula.

A = Child is nervous about being left with strangers.

B = A good mother deliberately exposes her children

to safe situations in which they're being cared for by people other than Mom so they become confident and self-reliant. A good mother knows children can handle the temporary stress and will feel increased self-esteem because of mastering the situation.

C = I feel happy about this opportunity to let my child increase his skills at playing with peers and learn he doesn't always need Mom.

Let's look at another situation I encounter frequently. Marilyn "can't stand" her husband getting angry with her. If he doesn't get his way about something, he always reacts with anger. Marilyn is so devastated by his anger she gives in and does what he wants.

When Marilyn came to counseling for depression, it didn't take long to discover the anger behind the depression. She can't always let her husband have his way, give in when she doesn't want to and hide her anger and frustration. There'll be repercussions from her repressed anger. Marilyn needs to take a look at her belief system and find some relief for her depressed feelings.

Let's put her problem in Ellis' ABC system.

A = Marilyn wants to join a Great Books Discussion Group that meets every Tuesday night at a member's home. Her husband, Ted, tells her he will not allow it. A wife should stay home in the evening, he tells her, looking grim and upset.

B = Marilyn believes when Ted gets mad at her he makes her life so miserable she hates it. Therefore she will do almost anything to avoid making him angry with her. Obviously she can't join the group.

C = Her feelings are frustration, disappointment and repressed anger, leading to depression.

We'll leave A the same, but let's change B and see what happens.

Marilyn might believe married couples don't always agree on everything. Each has a right to his or her feelings, but neither has the right to control the other. If Ted gets angry, Marilyn knows she *can* stand it. Eventually he'll realize he can't control her with his anger. Of course she'll join the group.

Her feeling is now eager anticipation about the group. She feels joy in the strength of being able to make her own decisions. She also feels happy with her discovery she won't be manipulated by her husband's anger.

This simple ABC formula has helped me many times in coping with problems I've had to work through. Frequently we see many beliefs we can choose from. It's a question of which beliefs we can follow.

Examining Our Beliefs

Sometimes it's simple to decide which beliefs to keep. I will keep some of my basic beliefs forever because they make good sense. They hold up in the light of logic. "Be honest." "Don't cheat." "Don't steal." Even with these, we could probably conjure up some exceptions. Maybe it's permissible for me to steal something if my child is starving and I'm penniless. She will surely die if I don't steal a slice of bread. But by and large, mine are reasonable beliefs to hold. I trust the ABC system to help me make decisions about my behavior. I haven't found a flaw in it yet.

Let's try a question that occurs to most of us at some time or other.

A = Pretend I'm becoming enamored with a tall, craggy, gentle, sensitive man. Toss in a British accent, while we're at it. Make him a millionaire besides, with a real castle! He's a widower and lonely, and he's mad about me. I might find myself enjoying his advances and flirting a little. I may eventually begin to ponder the ramifications of an honest-to-goodness affair. Let's look at my belief next.

B = I'm a happily married woman. An extramarital affair is wrong. It's unfair to my husband. I would hate myself if I ever had one.

C = My consequential feeling might be disappointment at being "cheated" out of what sounds like an exciting prospect in my life.

I examine my belief again, hoping desperately I'll find something I could change to give me permission to indulge myself. I might spend weeks examining it, but I can find no discrepancy. I'm stuck with my belief. I accept it, tell my shining knight we'll just have to be friends, and that's the breaks.

I can't change my belief if it makes sense to me. Even if a good salesman shows me why it must be wrong, outdated, irrational and inconsiderate, when it rings true, it rings true. I choose to keep my belief.

But suddenly I have another thought! What if I went ahead and had the affair! "What a good idea," I exclaim to myself. "I really want this knight, and to hell with my noble beliefs." Brazen hussy that I am, I rush to the phone to dial the castle. But as I hear the phone ringing, I realize if I go against my belief, I'll feel only regret and guilt.

Those feelings are so uncomfortable to me that I don't want to be stuck with them. I have a choice to go against my beliefs. But I decide to replace the receiver before my knight gets to his royal phone. Along with a little wistful regret, I feel a great sense of rightness and relief. For me, that's the best decision.

Let's explore an old-fashioned word I learned as a child but one I hear very rarely these days—*sin*. The best definition I've heard for sin was from my friend Kendra, who said, "Sin is anything that's bad for me." Period. That's it. Simple. I've found it to be true in any light I've looked at it under so far. That could apply to my getting drunk or binging out on chocolate peanut clusters.

Chocolate peanut clusters are my biggest weakness. It's all I can do to walk past them when they're on sale for $1.98 a pound. A sale price appeals to my sense of frugality. Coupled with my inordinate lust for them, it makes it nearly impossible to refuse.

Sometimes I walk past firmly and after a few yards, spin around, dive into my purse for money and hand it to the girl with trembling fingers and dry lips. When she gives me the peanut clusters, I might as well sit down on the curb and eat them right there. I know I'll eat them all in a very short space of time. My eyes glaze with joy, and I eat and eat and eat. When they're gone, my mouth feels thick with sugar, my tummy feels queasy, and my blood sugar begins to do uncomfortable things. In a few hours, I know I'll feel grouchy and lightheaded, not to mention *fat*.

Now that has got to be sin! I did something that was bad for me. Not overly serious, to be sure, but a good example of Kendra's definition. So for me, sin would be eating too much candy, drinking too much wine, lying, having an affair or anything that would make me dislike myself and feel regretful. Try that definition of sin on your own decisions.

Most of the time I prefer to behave so I won't feel guilty

and unhappy with myself. The peanut clusters are my most common moral lapse. But I believe I have the right to enjoy whatever *feelings* come my way.

Dealing With Other Feelings

I find myself attracted to men from time to time, and I enjoy it immensely. I used to feel guilty when that happened. Again I have Bill McCartin to thank for some good insight. He said, "It would be nice to think after people are married they would never again be attracted to another person. But that's not usually the way we work.

"Instead of trying to push away attraction when you feel it, concentrate more effort and attention on your spouse. Be a little nicer. If you appreciate your husband a little more, the other man will lose some of his luster. If you try to stop thinking of the other man, you'll just think of him more instead of less. Allow yourself the feelings of attraction. Don't try to shut them out. But don't *do* anything about them. Focus on your husband."

I've had several occasions to test his theory, and it's worked every time for me. But I still enjoy the feelings of attraction when it happens. It makes me feel warm, excited and energized. For me, that's enough. Larry gets the benefit of those feelings, and we're both happy.

Another "McCartinism" is his saying, "Love is not like jam, of which there's just enough to spread on one piece of toast. We have an endless amount of love, enough to keep spreading and spreading and never run out."

Again, I believe him. I've found I can love, genuinely *love*, many people, male and female. Sometimes my eyes fill with tears at the intensity of love I feel for a friend.

There's no problem with my having women friends because society encourages that. Unfortunately, there is still a problem with having friends of the opposite sex because society distrusts that.

Larry takes women out to lunch because he is a salesman for TV commercial time. Most TV-time buyers are women, and Larry does a lot of business over lunch. That was fine with me. But I always felt a little sorry for myself because I never got to have lunch with men. I find men delightful! And why, I wondered, was it OK for me to have lunch with Carolyn and Joyce but never to darken the doorway of a restaurant with Paul or John?

Every few months I'd bring up the subject. Larry always assured me that's how things go, that's all. It just wouldn't be proper. I'd argue awhile then quietly accept my fate for a few months. Then I'd mention it again, with the same results.

Finally, a few years ago, Larry conceded I was right. Logically, I should be able to go to lunch with men as well as with women. I was overjoyed, elated and eager to try my new lifestyle.

Guess what. I can't find men to lunch with! I began spreading the word far and wide I was now available for lunch. No one made an overture. After a few weeks, I added the fact I would certainly go Dutch, thinking maybe they were afraid I'd be an expensive date. Still no takers. Shaken by my dismal failure, with all my eager expectations dashed to the ground, I finally talked my husband's best friend into having lunch with me. His wife had no objection at all.

I'll call him "Dave" because even now I think he prefers no one know we ever lunched together. We agreed to meet at noon at a busy restaurant. I got there first (you might guess) and chose a table right by the door so he'd find me quickly. His jaw dropped when he saw me there. He said, "Don't you think we should sit someplace not so obvious?"

"Dave," I reasoned, "if we were up to no good we *would* hide. This way it's obvious everything is on the up-and-up."

But Dave was miserable. He kept one eye on the door the entire time, watching anxiously for people who might know him and think the worst. From time to time he called someone over and introduced me. "Frank! Frank, this is my best friend Larry Schnebly's wife. Larry and I have been best friends for years. Lee and Jan are friends, too. We all go to the same church!"

It wasn't nearly as much fun as I thought it would be. That was several years ago. I can count on one hand the male lunch partners I've had. They or their wives are simply too uncomfortable about it.

But I can't blame them because society has taught us a belief that most of us have accepted. If you get friendly with a person of the opposite sex, sooner or later it will lead to sex. To which I say a resounding, "Baloney!" I know I can like a whole bunch of people to the point of actually loving them. But I have never gone to bed with anyone but my husband. When temptation knocks, which it does, it doesn't take me long to realize I'd better not open the door. But how I love the feeling!

Replacing Bad Feelings With Good Feelings

Sometimes we feel discouraged, afraid, anxious, guilty, angry or sad. We want to shake the feeling, but we seem unable to do it. I've found some ways to help get rid of the bad feelings and replace them with good ones. One is to search out the belief behind the feelings and see if I can change it. This changes the feelings as easy as pie. We've just looked at the one way that helps us do it—the ABC system.

I learned another formula from a colleague, Dr. Maxine Ijams. I use it frequently. She puts any uncomfortable feeling through four steps.

1. Where did this feeling come from?
2. What am I getting out of it?
3. How long do I want to keep it?
4. What am I going to put in its place?

Let's look at an example. Larry and I went to Phoenix on a business trip. I had looked forward to shopping at my favorite shopping center for 4 hours while he called on his clients. I don't remember the cause, but shortly before we reached the shopping center we got upset with each other. By the time I got out of the car, I was angry. I slammed the car door and stalked away haughtily, furious with him. I strode along the mall, unwilling to enjoy the store windows because I was too full of resentment to allow anything pleasant to occupy my mind. Suddenly I remembered Maxine's four steps and tried them.

1. Where did this feeling come from? From Larry, of course. From that rotten creep I just left and from his rotten attitude.

2. What am I getting out of it? Self-pity and maybe a little strength in the knowledge I'm not going to let him run my life. I also got a twisted pleasure in slamming the car door and showing him how mad I was. But I mostly got a discomforting feeling that was ruining my afternoon.

3. How long do I want to keep it? I gave that some

thought and decided 5 minutes would suffice. I knew I wasn't willing to let go of the anger right then, but I didn't want to waste this glorious 4-hour shopping trip feeling mad at Larry. Five minutes would be perfect. I looked at my watch.

4. *What am I going to put in its place?* That's easy. After 5 minutes I'll concentrate on the shops and pretty clothes.

I continued to walk along, frowning, consciously loathing Larry. I told myself over and over how fed up I was with him, how rotten he was, how furious I was. I gave it everything I had. The 5 minutes seemed to take an awfully long time. When I looked at my watch and saw I could stop, I couldn't help chuckling at the procedure. I was feeling pleased that now I was free to *enjoy* the day. It was the first time I'd used the system, and it worked. I've used it many times since then.

The hardest step to fill in, I've found, is the second one, "What am I getting out of it?" Sometimes it takes some real soul-searching to answer that, as it did after my mother died.

I knew I would go through the stages of grief everyone experiences after losing a loved one. I let myself feel each one. I let myself cry and be sad. I felt depressed when I found myself doing it, but once in awhile I found myself focusing endlessly on feeling sad and wishing the sadness would lift.

Every time I went into a fabric store, I seemed to be drawn to the paisley prints. I remember how Mama loved paisley. I fondled the various fabrics. One time the sadness I felt seemed overwhelming to me. I tried to swallow the lump in my throat and remembered the four steps.

1. *Where did this feeling come from?* From seeing the paisley prints that reminded me of Mama.

2. *What am I getting out of it?* A feeling of closeness with her. A reliving of the times we shopped together. A kind of "magic" we frequently use in grieving—if I grieve hard enough and long enough maybe Mama will come back.

3. *How long do I want to keep it?* Suddenly I could imagine what she'd say to me if she was there. "Why are you doing this? I enjoyed all those pretty fabrics for years, but now I don't need them anymore. Stop looking at fabrics for me, and go find some for yourself and make some pretty clothes. Now go!" I smiled at the thought and knew I didn't want to keep that feeling of sadness any longer at all.

4. *What am I going to put in its place?* I decided to find some gorgeous velvet and a knockout pattern. I focused my thoughts on creating something terrific.

Another time I used the process after my son Lyle had gotten a new 10-speed bike and had gone riding around town. I found myself beginning to worry after a couple of hours. I was uncomfortably aware of every siren I heard.

1. *Where did this feeling come from?* The newness of the situation, along with the fact I didn't know where Lyle was.

2. *What am I getting out of it?* Maybe "magic" again. If I worry enough, he'll be all right. And maybe the comfort of believing a good mother worries about her children, so I must be a good mother.

3. *How long do I want to keep it?* Not another minute.

4. *What am I going to put in its place?* I'm going to picture how I felt as a child in Winslow, riding my bike along a desert road, feeling free and happy. Then I'll picture Lyle riding along a road here enjoying the same wonderful

freedom. I'll picture him smiling, getting tanned, feeling real pleasure in his hard-earned possession.

It was a pleasant picture. I was immediately able to turn to my housework without worry. It's a good system for changing our feelings, and I recommend it strongly.

We can't always change our feelings, but it's much easier if we change our thoughts. With practice it gets easier all the time, like playing the piano, wearing contact lenses or making lemon-meringue pie. It's hard at first, but the more we practice the easier it gets.

We need to give ourselves the permission to feel any way we choose to feel. Sometimes I want to be sad and wallow in self-pity for hours. Sometimes I want to be angry at someone or something and let those angry feelings wash over me until they're spent.

Accepting Our Feelings

The more we can accept our feelings, the less likely they are to bother us. But when they do bother us, and when we wish we were feeling some other way, it's nice to know we can polish the skills required to achieve that frame of mind.

There is a choice we have at all times that we frequently ignore. *We can take the secure thought or the insecure thought.* A lot of us seem to choose the insecure one every time! Just think how happy we'd be if we reversed that habit and always took the happy one.

Suppose I'm walking by a bus stop, and as I pass, two ladies begin to whisper. My insecure thought might be, "Oh, dear, I wonder what they're saying about me. I'll bet my slip is showing, or I'm dragging a piece of toilet paper under my shoe. I'll bet they're laughing at this old coat or my terrible posture."

My secure thought could be, "I'll bet they're admiring my hair. Maybe one of them remembers me from a talk I gave someplace. Maybe they like my casual, comfortable look."

Actually, they're probably not even aware of my having walked by. But as long as I have no idea what they're really saying, I'm free to think pleasant thoughts instead of unpleasant ones.

It was just as easy to picture Lyle happily riding his bike as it was to see him being put into the ambulance on a stretcher. There is *always* a secure counterpart to every insecure thought we can conjure up. Heaven knows we can find a million insecurities to entertain! It's fun to practice finding the secure thoughts.

One sure-fire way to change bad feelings is to think of something funny. Any incident that made you laugh long and hard is worth its weight in gold to stash away and use anytime you need a lift. One that never fails for me is the toilet-plunger incident.

I'd told the family many times that after anyone uses the "plumber's friend" to unstop the toilet, he should hold it over the bathroom wastebasket while he carries it out of the house. The wastebasket can catch any water drips. Larry resisted my good advice every time! I would see him race through the house carrying the plunger upside down but with no drip-catching wastebasket underneath. I begged him not do it that way because I was positive he would drip on the carpet. He stoutly maintained not a drop touched the floor and continued doing it his way.

One night, I heard him go get the plunger. I leaped from my chair to follow him to the bathroom and try again to get him to do it the *right* way (mine). He looked up defensively from his plunging and said with more than a touch of irritation, "Look, I'll show you how it's done. I defy you to find one drop on the floor after I've gone out."

I watched as he spun the plunger over the toilet and explained, "I'm spinning off any remaining liquid. None will be left to drip as I leave. You watch!" Then he turned it upside down and, holding it high in the air, ran down the hall and through the kitchen, with me following closely behind, watching for just one drop to fall.

Lindsay watched with some fascination as he sat at the breakfast bar munching popcorn. He mused, "That's the poor man's version of the Olympic torch!"

His remark threw me into gales of laughter as I realized how the scene must have looked. Now whenever I want to stop feeling bad, all I need to do is picture that scene, hear Lindsay's comment, and I giggle. In case you're wondering, not one drop hit the floor. In the face of such evidence, I withdrew my case.

All of us have hundreds of silly incidents we laugh at. They're like money in the bank to change our thoughts and our feelings.

Offering Encouragement

Sometimes it's fun to look back at our lives and pick out the people who inspired us the most. We may even narrow it down to the most-inspirational person we've ever known. Look carefully at the qualities that person had. You can be sure he or she was not an angry person, not rigid or demanding, not negatively critical.

Those who inspire us most are almost always warm and accepting. They look for the best in us, and they comment on it frequently. They believe in us so much they help us believe in ourselves. If they see negative traits in us, they don't dwell on them as much as they dwell on the positive ones.

Dr. Oscar Christensen calls it the "Atta-Boy" syndrome. When he was a child growing up in a rural area, there was nothing he couldn't do because his uncle always said, "Atta boy, you can do it. Atta boy, there you go. Atta boy, I knew

41

you could do it." And Chris found he could! When someone truly believes in us, we can hardly fail.

I like to use the example of a baby learning to walk. If you're a parent, do you remember when your baby tried to walk? Picture the scene in your mind. You were down on your knees, arms outstretched, beaming proudly at Junior, who was teetering tentatively, wanting to let go of the coffee table yet leery of taking the big step. Your whole body language was one of encouragement. You reached your arms toward him. You said, "Come on," invitingly, with such conviction he couldn't resist trying. When he fell you helped him up, but again you encouraged him to try because you knew he could do it. And he did!

Encouragement makes believers of us all!

I'm a pretty good pianist. I credit a lot of my skill to my family, who always knew I would be good at it. When we'd visit Grandma, who had a piano, I was always at the keyboard fooling around. It drove Grandma to distraction, but my parents said proudly, "Leona has a real talent for the piano!" I felt proud, positive that Paderewski had nothing on me. I continued to "play" by the hour. Finally, probably out of desperation, Grandma shipped the piano to our house. I began to take lessons from a music student at the local college. Because it was 1940, my teacher Kathleen charged only 50¢ an hour. She also kept telling me I could do it.

In addition to a beginner's book of notes and time values, she brought me Beethoven's "Fur Elise." We began at once on the first measure. To be playing a real piece immediately made me terribly proud. I knew Kathleen wouldn't have given it to me if she hadn't thought I could learn it. So

I learned it. I got more attention for playing the piano than anything I'd ever done before, so I played for hours on end. It's still an important part of my life.

I suspect I might have developed similar skills in almost any area if I'd been given the encouragement I got for playing the piano.

Probably everyone can look back and find someone who encouraged him in some way that had a profound effect in developing a particular skill.

On the other hand, we may be weak in some areas because we were *dis*couraged. I remember wanting to go to camp with my friend Donna when we were 10. Donna was a seasoned Girl Scout and raved about camp so much I also wanted to go. When I broached the idea to my mother, she scoffed. "You'd be scared to death and homesick," she declared and turned back to her pie making. I probably had some misgivings of my own because I dropped the issue pretty quickly, believing I was not put in this world to go to camp.

To this day I am not a camper. Why? I've never been to camp.

I wonder if I would be any different if my mother had encouraged me that day. She might have said, as she rolled out the dough, "You know, that might be fun for you! Especially with Donna along, you could have the time of your life! You'd swim and sleep in tents and see beautiful scenery and learn crafts. Oh, you might be a little homesick the first night, but not for long. You'd get over that and have a terrific time!" It makes such a difference when someone we value believes in us. Maybe I would have had the courage to go, and maybe I'd have loved it.

When I stop and think of the things I do well, I remember encouragement along these lines most of my life. "Leona is really a fast reader!" "Our Leona is an artist." "Lee is going to be a good seamstress. She can sew a dress in the time it takes me to lay out the pattern!" People pointed out my strengths, and I puffed with pride and got better and better.

Isn't it exciting to realize we might have the same effect on any number of people we see from day to day? To comment on a skill or attitude we admire in someone helps encourage them.

Unfortunately, society has taught us to *diminish* in the name of teaching. We think we need to point out people's mistakes or flaws for them to improve themselves. Teachers mark wrong answers with giant red check marks and they take the correct answer for granted. Traditionally, they wrote "9 wrong" at the top of the page instead of "41 right!"

I'm happy to see the tide turning as more teachers use positive comments. They encourage their students, rather than discouraging them.

We may try to be encouraging to our children, but we usually draw the line with adults. We usually believe adults are supposed to know how to do things right. But if we remember a misbehaving person is a discouraged person, it's easy to find discouraged people around us all day long! What fun it can be to use a little encouragement on them. It has to be sincere, of course, but we can always find something that's complimentary *and* sincere.

The first person who comes to mind is your spouse or mate or lover or what-have-you. What a glorious opportunity we have to try encouragement with him or her and watch the results at close range!

Real encouragement is given even when a person fails. It's given simply for the effort or just because the person is there.

My 26-year-old Lisa still glows as she recounts the joy she felt when she was about 10. She and I were on a Saturday afternoon shopping trip. I said to her with genuine warmth, "You know, Lisa, you're as much fun to be with as Shirley Nelson." Shirley was my adult friend. Lisa felt 10-feet high to be included in such lofty company. That compliment meant more to her than any others I ever gave her. And it wasn't for an achievement. It was just letting her know I liked her.

Encouragement helps people *know* they're worthwhile.

Encouragement? Praise?

There's a big difference between encouragement and praise. Sometimes it's hard to determine which is which. One of the basic differences is *praise* focuses on the product. *Encouragement* focuses on the process.

In other words, if Lindsay digs a hole so I can plant my new palo verde tree and I say, "That's a perfect hole you dug," that's praise. Encouragement would comment on the digging process rather than the hole. That's even better than praise. "I really appreciate your digging that hole for me. That's gotta be hard work." This says nothing judgmental about the quality of the hole but appreciates the digging of it. Whether the hole is perfect or imperfect, Lindsay has gotten my message of encouragement.

Unfortunately, I have been known to say things like, "Lindsay, how could you possibly think that hole would hold a tree? Any dummy could see it has to be twice that big!" That's classic *discouragement.* The next time I need a tree planted, I'll need to find someone besides Lindsay. We can imagine years hence Lindsay's wife pleading for a hole to be dug, and Lindsay muttering darkly, "I can't dig holes."

While praise is difficult to give in the face of failure, encouragement is easy. If Larry doesn't make his expected sales quota one month, I can't praise him. But I can encourage him by saying, "You *are* a good salesman, and you worked really hard at it. I can tell you're discouraged, but maybe next month will be better. Anyway, you're *my* favorite salesman any day!"

The encouraging person tries to help a person view life a little differently, more positively, more confidently. We must be cautious, however, not to be manipulative in our encouragement. Those vibes are bound to be felt by the manipulatee.

If I deliberately encourage Laurie in her poetry writing because I want a poet in the family, she'll sooner or later feel a kind of pressure to perform. She may back off from the possibility of not measuring up to my expectations. Better to encourage her in whatever interests she may explore and give her a constant acceptance, no matter what she decides to pursue.

Remarks like, "You look so happy when you're drawing, Laurie. You really enjoy it, don't you?" are encouraging in their attention. They also help her be aware of experiencing happy feelings as she draws. On the other hand, praise is a remark like, "That's a beautiful boat you've drawn, Laurie."

If Laurie leans toward perfectionism, she may be reluctant to try to draw another picture. If it isn't beautiful, she would have disappointed me. Praise imposes a "should" on people. Encouragement leaves them free to expand or change their skills and still feel worthwhile.

The child who is assured of his ability *to decide* is given a great gift. If Lindsay is trying to decide whether or not to buy a car, I can listen to the pros and cons of the venture. I have many choices of further responses, from the totally discouraging to the encouraging.

Discouraging statements include, "You'd be a complete idiot to buy that car. You know you could never keep up the payments. You've never finished anything you started. When are you going to start having some sense?" Encouraging remarks include, "Lindsay, you're good at making decisions. Whatever you decide to do, you'll find a way to work it out. You've always been so sensible. I'm impressed with how you usually seem to do the right thing."

Encouraging comments tell him he is smart and capable, and I believe in him. He continues to make wise decisions. He might make a bad decision from time to time, like getting in over his head and perhaps having to sell the car or take on another job. But that's all part of learning and building up a store of information for the next decision.

We're Not Responsible for the World

Many of us feel responsible for the whole world's behavior. We feel a need to point out all the ramifications and pros and cons of any subject. We throw in some advice when someone we know is trying to make a decision. *If* we're asked for our opinions, we should give them. But most advice is unasked for and largely unappreciated. Sometimes it comes across as discouragement, as though we have no faith in the person we're advising.

Parents are experts at telling their children ad nauseum what they should do, over and over, as though the children don't hear it the first time. Encouragement, on the other hand, is giving an opinion—once! You might say something like, "I'm sure you'll make a good decision," leaving it in their hands. An encourager believes in other people's abilities. The discourager believes he is the only one with the right answer.

We must try to avoid communicating encouragement with qualifiers. "You did a good job cleaning up after dinner, *but* you never remember to clean the sink." "Your hair looks nice, *but* you're wearing too much eye makeup again." "You got four A's, *but* what is this C doing here?" To be truly encouraging, leave off the qualifiers. Simply state the positive remark, and stop talking! Encouragement, not discouragement, is the catalyst for change.

You Can Be an Encourager

One very encouraging thought is—*If only ONE person believes in me, I can make it!*

Sometimes in counseling I see clients who are totally defeated. They've been put down, criticized, scolded, laughed at and bawled out until they've come to believe they simply don't measure up. They're discouraged to the bone, and their behavior usually shows it. Frequently they're misbehaving in some way. Alcoholism, chronic loss of temper, hypochondria, aggressiveness, passiveness, depression and other kinds of behavior trouble them or the people around them.

One of my roles as a therapist is to *encourage*. While we look for the causes and payoffs of a problem, I encourage my client's abilities and strengths. It's easy to do because I genuinely believe in him! I never fake it. I don't have to because I *know* he has strengths. All I have to do is help him find them.

Sometimes I'm the first person who has believed in him for years. A client is almost reluctant to believe me. But the evidence of his own worth is there. He can't deny it. I believe in him, in his ability to change, to grow, to be positive. Soon he believes in himself.

Look at some of the discouraged people you know. Could you be one of the people who will cause changes in their lives because you believe in them? It takes only one person, and you might be that one!

One way we discourage, without intending to, is by doing things for someone. I don't recommend selfish behavior or refusal to help each other. I suggest you avoid falling into the trap of overdoing. Overprotecting and overdoing can be more harmful than neglect.

When we do too many things for our children or for other adults, we may be saying in effect, "You can't do it. You aren't able. I have to do it for you." In our eagerness to love, nurture, help or teach, we actually end up discouraging. Those we try to help may come to believe they *can't* do it. In their dependence on us, they become weaker. We diminish them by "loving" too much. That kind of love is frequently not love at all but a kind of ego trip. The doer enjoys feeling "needed" and superior.

I remember a friend of ours who was the only child of a widow. The mother was a proverbial "saint" and did everything to make young Bill happy. She walked with him to

school every day for years so he wouldn't be picked on by
bullies or attacked by dogs. If there were school field trips,
she volunteered to go along as a chaperone so she could be
with her son in case he needed her. She baked him something fresh and tantalizing every day. When school was out,
the two of them sat and ate warm gingerbread or chocolate-
chip cookies and talked over his day. The sun rose and set
on Bill. Mom reveled in his need for her. She got a lot out
of being necessary for his very existence, as she saw it, so
she continued her behavior for years. All the time Bill was
getting the message he couldn't survive in this world
without Mom.

Tragically, Mom was killed in an accident when Bill
was in high school. He almost *didn't* survive without her
because Bill had never learned to be strong and self-suffi-
cient. He had to have a lot of intensive therapy before he
could begin to believe in himself.

Most of us aren't that smothering, but frequently we
use the same discouraging dynamics in little ways. As parents we need to remember the purpose of being a parent—
to make our children self-reliant, happy, strong, capable
people. The best way we can do that is to encourage!

Encouraging can also be used in other types of relationships. I saw a young couple, Don and Janet, in my office.
They were going together. They had the unusual wisdom to
seek counseling even though they weren't married. Don had
a bad problem with jealousy, and Janet had trouble with his
anger. Together they had woven a tangled web of unhealthy
dynamics beginning with his jealousy when she talked to
another man. He got furious with her. She became so upset
at his anger that she cried and withdrew.

This had become such a common pattern in their relationship they developed secondary problems. To avoid his jealousy and resultant anger, Janet stopped talking to boys at all. But she resented Don's "making" her give up all male friends. While he appreciated her efforts, Don found her coldness and obvious resentment toward him very uncomfortable. And he didn't like himself much for manipulating her into giving up so many friends because of his insecurities.

They understood the dynamics very well, but they didn't know how to stop the habit patterns they were in. Through the use of encouragement they gradually changed their own behavior and were delighted at how well it worked. Janet gently encouraged Don to allow her to talk to boys, even though he felt threatened when he saw it. Don felt angry and scared, but he was determined to lick it. He was willing to face discomfort if it helped him learn to live with his feelings in a healthier way.

Janet told Don, "I know you were a little upset when I was talking to Stan at lunch. But I was so happy to see you controlling it and letting me talk to him in spite of your feelings. I really appreciate that!" Her encouragement helped him continue the struggle that was so difficult for him.

On the other hand, Don encouraged her in "standing" his anger when he gave into it. When he felt overwhelmed by the threat of losing her and the old habit of anger reared its ugly head, he yelled if he wanted. She told herself she could stand it. She waited until it subsided, or she refused to listen to his tirade and left. She stopped responding with tears as she had in the past. When Don cooled down, he complimented her on how well she had tolerated his anger.

Both were keenly sensitive to each other. The encouragement they gave and got helped them grow stronger and overcome these problems in their relationship. They might have accomplished the same results without the encouragement but not as pleasantly. Encouragement reinforces good behavior while accepting the bad. Encouragement oils the wheels of positive change.

Coping With Sexual Attitudes

Cinderella never had sex. She got all dressed up, went to the ball and charmed the socks off the handsome prince, who whisked her off to the castle. Then for the rest of their lives, he worshipped her, agreed with her, hugged her often, kissed her tenderly, held her close as they talked hour after hour, chuckled warmly at her cute ways and made her happy. She was the princess. He was the prince put into this world to make her happy ever after!

Though that concept may be a bit ridiculous, many women unconsciously expect marriage to be that way. Most of us were totally unaware of the expectations our husbands had been entertaining. While we were fantasizing about being Cinderella in the castle, the boys were busy with their own fantasies. In theirs, Cinderella was a real sexpot. She couldn't wait to hop off the horse, race the prince to the castle garret and begin an outrageous strip-tease to the tune of Harlem Nocturne. That was only the beginning of the passionate sex life they would enjoy forevermore, in which she couldn't keep her hands off his body. She would be his own Playboy bunny—aggressive, seductive and sultry. She would combine these traits with others that would be helpful to his career. She would also be a gourmet cook. A kind of combination Farrah Fawcett and Julia Child.

Because today's young wives see love, sex and marriage far differently from the way their mothers viewed them, we might think young women sail into marriage with nary a misconception. But alas, it doesn't work that way. Cinderella and the prince live on in a never-ending clash of "shoulds" that both partners still bring to the wedding.

Understanding Our Expectations

Our expectations are part of the problem. One is the old appeal of forbidden fruit. All of us want what we can't have, and conversely often we *don't* want what we *should* have. Recently, a bride of less than a year poured out her hurt and confusion in my office. "Tom and I couldn't get enough sex before we were married. We slept together the first night we met and several times a day after that. We lived in his apartment for 4 months before the wedding. Our sex life was unbelievable. But right after we got married, he cooled almost immediately. Now he hardly touches me anymore."

Tom said, "If Margie would just quit hounding me for sex, I probably would want her again. But by now it's such a big 'should' that it's no fun. The more she nags me, the more I turn off."

Tom and Margie came from religious homes. Both felt guilty even while they enjoyed their fantastic premarital sex. Once it was approved, it lost much of its appeal for Tom. Some people love a challenge, and when the challenge goes, so does the lust. Furthermore, it became a power struggle to each of them. Each tried to make the other behave in the way they "should."

Couples who remain virgins until the marriage bed sometimes feel disappointed after "saving" themselves all that time while they read about the fireworks that awaited them. Sometimes the actual experience doesn't measure up to the almost-unbearable ecstasy they imagined. They feel cheated, discouraged and angry with each other.

"It just isn't as exciting as I thought it would be," they say.

The very intimacy of marriage can also detract from sexual desire. The dashing young man who visits Pam in her singles apartment is pure excitement with his flowers, gifts and bottles of good wine. The scent of his shave lotion thrills her, as does his sparkling conversation and even the tone of his voice. His touch is magic and his gaze electric. Simply being in his presence is an automatic turn-on. The thrill of his kisses makes him totally irresistible. The physical attraction is constant and insatiable.

Then comes the wedding and the total togetherness and the beginning of disillusionment. Pam begins to resent little habits she wasn't aware of before. She misses the flowers, gifts and bottles of wine. There are few surprises anymore. There's criticism, arguing and disapproval. His touch is no longer an automatic turn-on but a demand. She bristles at it sometimes.

Though the pilot light is not necessarily out, it is definitely flickering.

Our grandmothers used to say, "Familiarity breeds contempt." Only determined couples can keep sex fun and exciting in spite of constant familiarity. Most of us thought it would be fun and exciting forever, or we wouldn't have agreed to marry in the first place. Is there a solution? I don't think so.

Maybe disillusionment is part of a giant Master Plan to keep civilization going. Maybe we need our naive attitude of hope and expectation or no one would ever marry. But whether or not we need it, I'm convinced we'll always have it. Hope springs eternal.

So our expectations cause us some disappointment. So what? Sex is no different from anything else. As we live and grow, we discover many expectations can cause us disappointment. It's one of those lessons we learn only by experiencing it frequently enough.

Our Needs Vary

Another problem in sexuality is the variety of different needs we have. So many disenchanted young wives tell me, "All he thinks about is sex! I want to be held and kissed and hugged. But for him it always leads to the bedroom. I want *love*, but he just wants *sex*."

The husbands look confused and say, "Isn't that what marriage is for? Of course I want sex. Adults who love each other should want sex. I love my wife. I just can't understand her not wanting sex as much as I do."

I think they're both right. There's a lot of truth to the statement, "Men use love to get sex, and women use sex to get love." Of course women enjoy good sex, and men genuinely love their wives. But I think the thrust of their focus is biologically different.

Often a wife will express a wish to be simply held, "with no strings attached." She doesn't want sex but only a gentle tenderness that will make them feel close and loved. And the husband will shrug and say, "Well, sure, if that's all she wants. I can do that. I'll be glad just to hold her with no strings attached." And he means it sincerely. He loves his wife, and if it will make her happy he's glad to oblige.

Later that evening he joins her on the sofa just to hold her. She's delighted! She snuggles warmly and thinks, "This is what life is all about. Oh, this is lovely! I feel so warm and secure and content and loved." And just about then she feels his hand on her breast, hears his breathing get heavy and sees hunger in his eyes. A stab of resentment goes through her. He promised! He said no strings attached, and now he wants to go to bed. No fair! She pulls away in disappointment and sees the rejection and hurt in his face and feels guilty.

Sometimes she goes ahead with it, and they have sex. But she feels cheated of the pure, undemanding tenderness she had expected him to provide. Or she may refuse sex, and he feels rejected, unloved, hurt and angry. Either or both will end up unhappy.

So what happens? They may begin to avoid these situations to avoid the potential hurt. The wife may find any number of chores to do in the evening so she won't appear idle and inviting. Her husband may hesitate to make any overtures at all rather than risk rejection. They both feel like failures. But they're just two normal people with feelings like everyone else. The problem is one has a quicker turn-on point than the other.

It can work both ways. I've encountered more women who complain of overly ardent husbands. But many women complain their husbands won't turn on no matter how flimsy their nightgowns or how many hints they toss out.

I'm convinced one partner or the other always has a higher sex drive. So what's the big deal? Why is it any worse if one has a bigger appetite than the other?

It's all right for a couple to go to dinner and order what they want. For him, a giant slab of prime rib complete with baked potato, sour cream, fried zucchini, salad with roquefort dressing, garlic bread and apple pie with ice cream. For her, a chef's salad. We never question the difference in food appetites, but somehow we feel there's something wrong if our sexual appetites differ.

We believe if we really love each other we should both want to make love at the same instant, with the same regularity. And if we don't, we feel angry or guilty or hurt, or all three.

It seems to me the obvious solution is to think of sex the way we think of food. If Larry loves rice pudding every night and I don't, nothing prevents me from fixing it for him. I'll be glad to give him rice pudding frequently, if he wants it, as long as he doesn't insist I have some too. From time to time I might decide rice pudding looks pretty good, and I'll have a dish myself. But you can be sure if he *demands* rice pudding or lays a guilt trip on me because I don't want any, I may starve to death before I'll eat any. I may even stop providing it for him.

Some good friends of ours have been married for 35 years. They handle the "problem" of differing sexual appetites so well it never became a problem at all. They simply agreed years ago their only obligation to each other was to "be there." Frequently when one's desire is greater than the other's, both end up equally excited by just being there. If they don't, that's fine. One can be actively thrilled, and the other simply pleased at cooperating. Feelings don't get hurt and egos don't get shattered because neither has any expectations or "shoulds."

Not infrequently my clients, almost always the women, complain they feel "used." Trudy said, "I stay home with the kids all day, and my only contact with the outside world might be other women at a plastic-ware party or a neighbor's coffee. Mike is at a huge office full of people all day long. Some of the women he talks to are gorgeous. I know he likes them. I feel like he gets turned on by them all day long then comes home and expects me to satisfy all that desire. It's not love for me he's feeling just pure physical lust for something feminine. I'm supposed to be available. Not only available but willing and eager. Well, I'm sorry, but I'm not."

Mike denies the accusation, but his reassurances fall on deaf ears. It's possible Trudy is at least partly right because sometimes we do get excited by people other than our mates. We automatically turn to our mates without even questioning where the desire came from in the first place.

This won't be a problem if other things are going well.

If there's an atmosphere of love, respect and cooperation to begin with, the lovemaking feels natural and good to both parties. But if the communication and warmth are lacking, sex becomes questionable.

Sex Is Communication

Actually, sex is communication. When the communication is bad, sex is bad. When we improve our communication, we improve our sex lives.

Another fly in the ointment of sexuality is unexpressed resentment. I know from experience if I get angry with Larry and try to ignore it, pretend it isn't there and refuse to deal with it, I store up resentment until wild horses couldn't drag me to his arms. Until the issue is resolved, I will be a very reluctant bed partner, if I'm any at all. I'd be like my friend Betty who, when her husband makes unwelcome overtures, says, "Oh, you wanta play rent-a-corpse tonight?" Making love with a cold, grim wife is hardly rewarding, although lots of men prefer it to the alternative of no sex at all.

Another problem about unexpressed resentment is it increases the chance of an affair. The longer I withhold my feelings from Larry, the more appealing it becomes to share those feelings with someone else. I become vulnerable, and so does he. A kind, sensitive ear from someone else is often an irresistible invitation to something more. Actually, I use the word "irresistible" very loosely because I believe we *can* resist anything we want to resist. If we really want it, we just like to convince ourselves we "couldn't help it!"

Some people deliberately seek affairs to get even with

their mates, as Marsha did. "I resented him so long and so hard I had an affair just to show him I wasn't going to put up with his lack of attention. I wanted to hurt him badly. I knew it would hurt him more than anything else."

She was right. It did. The relationship was irreparably damaged, which was more than Marsha had intended.

Unresolved resentment takes its toll in a lot of other unsavory ways, including lack of desire and even impotence. When I work with an impotent husband, I almost always find some hostility toward his wife that needs to be resolved before the physical problem can be solved.

One husband maintained he couldn't have an erection with his wife, but he often awoke with one. Being able to have an erection at *any* time means impotence is not a physical impairment. We had to look at his relationship with his wife. Once we improved their communication and the quality of time they spent together, the impotence disappeared.

Unresolved resentment almost always interferes with good sex. People who are "pleasers," see page 122, need everyone's approval so much they don't express their irritations. They don't get angry. They get even. What better way to punish the offending spouse than by disinterest in sex?

The best solution to unresolved resentment is letting our feelings out. I *have* to tell Larry when I'm annoyed, disappointed or furious with him, even though I risk an argument or withdrawal or whatever made me reluctant to rock the boat in the first place. If I remind myself I can stand his disapproval and our relationship will benefit from my honest complaints, it helps me talk things out and get it over with. The longer I put off talking to him honestly, the longer I have no desire for closeness, warmth or sex.

Sex Is Power

Although sex is one of the last things that should ever become a power arena, it frequently does. Carol complains, "Sex seems like a victory to him. It's like he's *won,* and I've lost. Even when he does nice things, I can see he's really just trying a gimmick so I'll give in. And when I do give in, I feel horrible afterward. I lie there and cry. I wonder why it isn't beautiful and rewarding anymore. Instead I'm just a challenge to his manhood. He proves he's macho by making love to me."

Though Carol could be misinterpreting her husband's intentions, chances are she's partially correct. We feel other people's attempts at power, although sometimes we don't recognize it as such. We just know it makes us mad.

"Oughta wantas" are big in the sexual battleground. "You oughta wanta make love. Wives oughta wanta have sex," he says. She counters with, "You oughta wanta talk to me. You oughta wanta be close to me."

When each tries to control the other, nobody wins. Everyone loses in a power struggle. If you "win," it's only a temporary victory until the other party bests you. Yet tonight in millions of bedrooms around the world, people will compete, try to control one another and try to be more powerful by demanding or refusing sex.

The solution is to ask yourself if you're involved with that game. Sex and power can't survive simultaneously. Even in harmless games, like Monopoly or Scrabble, players often are sore losers. If you shoot for power in the bedroom, you automatically lose before you start.

How do you end the power struggle? One partner must be willing to withdraw from it. Share this insight with your partner, opening the subject for discussion. If that's too threatening, try changing your attitude, motivation and behavior.

Use Cooperation in Your Relationship

Competition and cooperation cannot coexist at the same time. A rich sexual relationship demands cooperation. If you tend to be a competitive person, you may be competing in your marriage or love relationship. If you are, your sex life is probably disconcerting. Make the decision to start cooperating instead. Treat your partner with respect, improve your communication and get out of the one-upmanship game.

Sue and Andy came for counseling because their sex life was not what they wanted. "Sue seems to have a plastic shield around her," Andy complained. "She's fine when we're out for the evening with other people. She seems warm and happy. She has a good time with me, until we reach our bedroom at home. Then she gets quiet, seems preoccupied and withdraws from me completely. She builds this wall around herself."

Sue nodded in agreement, with a very sad expression. She seemed to be taking the blame but couldn't help what she was doing and felt badly about it.

We talked at length about feelings and attitudes. Sue told of her biggest fear. "I'm scared to death of being abandoned or rejected. I'll never forget the day my father walked out on my mother and how we all cried. Mother never got over it because she and my father had always been close. It came like a bolt from the blue. We had all trusted my father, and we shouldn't have. He left us."

Sue's childhood decision was never to get into that bind herself. She avoided the risk by never getting too close to anyone.

But for sex to be good, there has to be trust. True, we're vulnerable when we trust. And some people prefer not take that risk.

In Sue's case we had to do some counseling before she became willing to take the risk. Once the decision was reached, she was able to let down her defenses and open up to Andy for the first time since they'd married.

Sometimes the reason for distrust is more recent and very clear. "I was married before, and my first husband wasn't trustworthy. He was fooling around with other women right from the start. Our marriage was just a handy place to come between affairs."

It's a fact there are no guarantees in this world. We're always vulnerable to deceit or a change of heart that could lead to rejection. If that happens, we can stand it. Yet a lot of people are reluctant to believe in anything that chancy. Ages ago someone said, "It's better to have loved and lost than never to have loved at *all*." But tell that to a recent divorcee and watch her expression of disdain.

It boils down to an individual decision, one we must all make for ourselves. Without a willingness to risk, to open up and be vulnerable, you'll never allow yourself to feel close to someone. Your sex life will be mediocre at best.

Personally, I highly recommend the risk. When you love someone, you are vulnerable. You'll be hurt from time to time, but it's worth it when you're able to enjoy a really intimate relationship.

Sexual Performance

Probably the all-time king-size problem in the sexual arena is performance. We worry about how our partner is going to evaluate us and whether or not we'll measure up to his or her expectations. What a shame anything so basic as sex has taken on so many fears of inadequacy. But it has. We experience fear of performance more than any other area of sexual dysfunction.

Debbie says plaintively, "The more educated we become, the more performance is demanded of us! It used to be that men were happy if their wives would just 'submit.' No more! Now they get upset and uptight if we don't have orgasms every time. Multiple orgasms, yet!

"They analyze our orgasms. My husband keeps asking, 'Did you have a vaginal orgasm or just a clitoral orgasm?' I'm sick of having my lovemaking analyzed all the time. I wish I could get away with 'just submitting' like my mother did!"

She has a realistic complaint. A husband may feel threatened if he can't send his wife into "webs of ecstasy," as a gothic novel might say. He is so concerned with perfection in lovemaking he may put pressure on his wife. This needlessly complicates the whole matter.

On a recent popular talk show, guests explained their research indicated women might be able to ejaculate during intercourse. While the largely feminine audience was interested in the presentation, one well-received comment was now men will have yet another goal to pursue—finding the "magic button" to push so women could ejaculate.

"They've taken the magic out of romantic love," sighed one lady. "It's become a scientific skill." Someone else suggested what we need is more candlelight and wine, and fewer charts to follow. There was a feeling men and women already have far too many "shoulds" about intercourse.

Perhaps the biggest culprit behind our performance fears is the monster of perfectionism. "If I can't do something perfectly, I'm not going to try it at all." That attitude is crippling enough in other areas to cheat us out of a lot of pleasure, from reluctance to try new sports or new skills like guitar playing to sex. But sex never has to be perfect to be enjoyable.

I love my friend George's statement, "When sex is good, it's just great. When sex is bad, it's still great!" George's wife is a lucky lady, with no pressures of performance and no expectations of perfection from her husband. George himself is equally lucky, with the freedom simply to enjoy and cooperate without measuring.

Once we start to measure the quality of our performance, we lose much of the pure pleasure we could be relishing. When we spend so much mental energy evaluating, we forfeit spontaneity.

But the worst penalty of perfectionistic evaluation is the fact we can *never* measure up! True perfection is impossible. We're doomed to a life of disappointment.

We need to lower our standards and apply the adage, "Have the courage to be imperfect." Quit worrying about performance. If you have to ask "How was it?" you're missing the whole point. As George says, "The worst sex I ever had was terrific!"

"Sex Education" for Adults

I'm not opposed to education, but I do think we might be taking sex education for adults a bit too seriously. There are thousands of cookbooks packed with hundreds of mouth-watering recipes, but no husband ever expected us to try them all. In fact, most are content with a basic pot roast, potatoes, vegetable, bread and dessert. They rarely ask, "Aren't you willing to try the pork-and-apple Oriental on page 68 of that new cookbook you got for your birthday?" And if any husband did ask, the answer would likely be a resounding, "Hell, no!" which would end the discussion then and there.

Not so with sex. "Dan says he and his wife read *The Delights of Sex* at bedtime and try a different page every night. Shall we do that?" Or "Honey, you're so conservative. There are hundreds of different positions. Why do you always want the same one or two or three?"

A wife might say, "My friend Julie can't wait till bedtime because Steve is so creative in his lovemaking. He thinks of such exciting erotic things to do she just can't get enough!" Or "I love reading those romantic novels because the sex scenes sound really fantastic. Why don't we make love that way?"

The resulting feelings are the same for both sexes —threat and inadequacy. "I must be a lousy lover. I'm dull, uncreative, stodgy. I'm a miserable failure and will avoid the whole thing," Another way of responding might be, "Damn it, if I'm not a good enough lover at home, I'll have an affair and prove I'm terrific." Regardless of which gender is complaining, the reaction is the same. "Maybe I can't measure up." So in self-defense, we attack each other.

"You know what you are? Frigid!"

"If you were a decent lover I'd be fine!" Then both partners feel threatened by their "poor performance," which in reality might be perfectly good.

We're the best-educated generation there ever was. A price we pay for it is the awareness anything can be improved. So we begin to feel inadequate. But education isn't the only cause. Plain old inferiority can also cause feelings of inadequacy.

"I have such small breasts. I'm ashamed to have my lover see them."

"I haven't had the experience most men have. How am I going to satisfy her?"

"I'm afraid I'll never be able to reach a climax. I'll die of embarrassment."

"I'm not big like a lot of guys."

The more we stew about it, the more apprehensive we become. Sometimes we're almost immobilized by feelings of inadequacy.

Morality and Our Sexual Attitudes

Another strong deterrent to our sexual enjoyment is the issue of morality. Even though we're adults and allowed to do all the things we couldn't wait to do "when we grow up," we're often stuck with the beliefs we formed as children. Many of the thoughts that plague us now are the result of attitudes our parents instilled in us, for our protection or our own good.

We still have little tape players in our minds. They play endless tapes of old "shoulds" and "shouldn'ts" that influence our behavior and feelings, even when we're not aware of it. Complicating the problem is the fact every one of us has different tapes. Yet most of us think our own beliefs are the "right" ones.

Women born in the 1930s knew zilch about sex. Our mothers blushed at the very mention of the word and could hardly explain the physical process to us, let alone the emotional dynamics. As little girls, we quickly learned our parts "down there" were not to be touched or looked at. My own mother tried hard not to overreact when she saw Betty and me "playing nurse" behind the oleanders. But her very manner and expression as she called us in for cookies indicated great discomfort and shame. When I copied my brother's phrase, "They caught me with my pants down," my mother called me aside and told me quietly it wasn't a nice thing for a girl to say.

We grew up filled with doubts about the appropriateness of our sexuality. Each of us had to struggle with making our own codes and beliefs just as much as older women, though perhaps in different ways.

Rick and Donna came in with a disagreement about mateswapping. Donna said, "He wants to swap with our friends. I just can't bring myself to make love with that other guy."

I went into my theory that nobody should have to do anything they aren't morally comfortable with. Donna interrupted, "Oh, it's not that I think it's *wrong*. I like to sleep with other men. It's just that one guy I can't stand."

It was good for a chuckle. It was also a clear indication we all have different moral standards.

One moral code everybody agrees on, though, is the fact sex between husband and wife is perfectly appropriate and desirable and is to be enjoyed. It seems we shouldn't have problems in that area, yet we do.

"He'd like oral sex, and I think it's wrong."

"I'm ashamed I have fantasies about other men while I'm having intercourse with my husband."

"I feel guilty about using birth control because of my religion, so I never really enjoy sex."

"Even though I know it's all right now that I'm married, I still somehow feel dirty doing it."

"Sex with girl friends and prostitutes is one thing. But I feel like my wife is so good and pure I can't get turned on to her."

"I'm so dependent on my husband he feels like a father figure. It seems incestuous to make love with him."

How do we deal with these moral dilemmas? Communication. We need to talk to our mates and express our fears, doubts and concerns. We can consult many other sources for education and reassurance—our priests, ministers, rabbis, marriage counselors. Even books on the subject help us make our decisions.

In the end, making decisions is up to us. We can draw on all kinds of sources, but we have to decide for ourselves what we believe is right and wrong.

Once we determine what we believe, we have to *do* it— or *not* do it, as the case may be. Changing our beliefs doesn't automatically change our feelings in a jiffy. It takes time to get used to new beliefs and feelings.

If I decide I want to turn over a new leaf and become wildly erotic, experimenting with all sorts of sexual play, I have to give myself permission first. Then I have to plunge in and try it, even if I feel embarrassed and uncomfortable. Only by *doing* it will my feelings begin to change. Soon I may find myself really enjoying all the new behavior, but I won't ever enjoy it unless I start.

New feelings and behavior have to come from our own decision that we *want* to change, and that we believe it's OK. If someone else is trying to get me to change while I truly believe such behavior is wrong, I'll probably never enjoy it. It just won't work.

What do we do in a case like that? If one person in the marriage thinks oral sex is terrific and the other thinks it's dreadful, all we can do is approach the problem like any other problem. Try compromise and negotiation along with communication. "I'm willing to try oral sex if you'll paint the porch." Or "Gee, honey, in spite of all the books that encourage it and even though Father Doyle says it's fine, I still can't bring myself to do it. I'm really sorry . . . I guess we'll never be perfectly matched in every way, will we? But remember, even the worst sex is terrific!"

Other Sexual Problems and Solutions

There are other problems in our sexual endeavors that may seem relatively unimportant. But they can be disheartening nonetheless.

"I'm a night person, and he's a morning person. He falls asleep even before I get my teeth brushed, so we never get to make love at night. Then in the morning, he's grabbing for my parts while I'm still sound asleep. I get upset with him."

Solution? Compromise. "Two nights a week we make love and two mornings a week." Or "This week we do it at night. Next week we do it mornings." That's fair and respectful.

"Sex is boring. Always exactly the same." Sonia and Tim made up fantasies to tell each other and acted out the ones that were feasible. Kate and Geoff checked into the NoTell Motel for a night. Tina and Chuck tried a few X-rated movies. Molly and Michael bought books on variation and technique. Boring sex is easy to liven up when both parties are willing to experiment.

Another common complaint is "I'm so afraid of getting pregnant I can't relax." That's a very real problem and one I won't try to solve. All you can do is investigate the different kinds of birth control that are available and to find which is best for you. Take solace in the fact you'll eventually be past menopause. You'll never have to worry again. There *are* some advantages to age!

"I'm so aware of the kids. I hear every little sound. I can't relax and enjoy sex when one of them is crying or calling for me."

That's a tough one. Generally mothers are more in tune with their children's sounds because they spend more time taking care of them. It's difficult to turn off that feeling of responsibility. It's harder to let ourselves get into a sexual experience when we hear a child crying for us.

Here we need to consider frequency. If children are in the habit of crying or yelling for you often at night, you need to change your response pattern. If a child is in genuine need, you'll probably have to shatter the loving mood and go tend to him. Hopefully you can get the loving feelings back afterward.

I encourage parents to start closing their bedroom doors when their children are very young. You'll still be able to hear them if they cry or call out in need. But they'll grow up with the knowledge parents enjoy privacy. Most parents leave the door open so they'll be able to hear what's going on. This can cause problems when the kids get older.

Mary Lou said, "As soon as Jim and I close the door to our bedroom, the kids gather right outside in the hall. They ask for snacks and wonder what we're doing. We can't relax with that going on!"

Indeed they can't. Children should learn at an early age that parents need to be alone. But if you can't bring yourself to close your door all night every night, close yourselves in for short periods on a regular basis. Leave orders you're not to be disturbed unless it's an emergency. You don't have to make love every time, but you get the kids used to your privacy together so it will be accepted and taken for granted.

It's also good modeling for them. They'll know *they* deserve privacy when they're grown up and married.

Sexual Appetites Vary

The most common problem I encounter is the variance in sexual appetites. The best solution is compromise. One couple who solved it beautifully were Janet and Vince.

Janet has a fairly low sex drive, while Vince seemed to think about nothing else. When I asked him how often they thought they'd like sex if it were up to them, Janet piped up, "Once a month," just as Vince was saying, "Three times a day!"

What they did was find a number in between the two extremes. It took a lot of communication and discussion. Their reasoning was so skilled it would have made any debate team sit up and take notice. But they finally settled on "every 4 days."

It was considerably more often than Janet would have liked. But the agreement included the fact she could lie there and think about anything she wanted during the process because Vince was the one who "needed" sex. Because they really loved each other and wanted to cooperate, the solution was fine.

Another couple had the same problem in reverse. Jennifer was the physically affectionate one. Bill was relatively disinterested. In their case, we added manual stimulation, a vibrator. Jennifer was the one who wanted orgasm frequently, so she was delighted to have him apply the vibrator. In no time at all she reached a climax. Granted, it wasn't the proverbial "web of ecstasy," but it was satisfying nonetheless. Bill agreed he would satisfy Jennifer twice a week by whatever means he chose. He used the vibrator when he didn't feel like getting more involved himself.

Some people object to compromise and negotiation in sex on the grounds it takes the joy and spontaneity out of romance. It makes sex a business agreement instead of an act of love. But the people who are willing to try it generally find it solves their problems. As I said before, once we get involved we often find ourselves turning on after all.

Although sex is important, it is *not* the most important

thing in marriage. Sometimes we can get so focused on our Sexual Problems we lose sight of all the good things we have going for us. If you can take the pressure off by using some of these suggestions, do it. But recognize the fact sex alone doesn't determine the quality of a relationship.

I know many couples who deeply love each other. The joy they find in being together is beautiful to see. They have common interests, mutual respect and senses of humor that keep the marriage well-nourished. They have varying degrees of sexual incompatibility, but they accept those the way people accept any other problems in life. They make the best of the good things they have going for them.

I've known other couples who had superb sex lives. They enjoyed sex all the way to the divorce court because there wasn't much else in their relationship.

I don't know of any couple who has a perfect sex life. We all have problems in that area. So if you have sex problems, isn't it nice to know you're normal? Relax and join the club.

Dealing With Behavior

Have you ever heard yourself say, "I just can't understand why Jerry acts that way. It simply escapes me. He *knows* I hate it when he does things like that." Perhaps it's a husband, a parent, one of your children or a neighbor who has you at loose ends. Anytime we find ourselves annoyed at another's behavior, no matter what it is, we can begin to understand it more easily if we can figure out its purpose.

Alfred Adler said all behavior has a purpose or it wouldn't exist. If I get up to get a glass of water, certainly there is a purpose for it—I'm thirsty. Or I need an excuse to leave my typewriter. Or I want to stretch my legs. Or I have to take an aspirin. There has to be a reason, or I wouldn't be going for water.

The same logic works for everything we do in life. We always have a purpose for doing it. Finding that purpose helps us deal with our behavior and behavior we're trying to understand in others. Every person is goal-oriented. Some-times we disguise our goals so cleverly it's difficult to dis-cover what we're really hoping to accomplish.

Depression is a good example. It is always a silent tem-per tantrum. We don't feel depressed without first having some anger we don't recognize or deal with effectively. We refuse to admit to being angry because "nice people don't get angry" or "of course I can't get mad at Mama" or what-ever the reason. So we must do *something* with that anger. When we don't let the anger out, we turn it in. At that point, it can become depression.

When I deal with a depressed person, I try to help him find the source of his anger. Often a client says, "Oh, no, I'm not angry, just depressed." Sometimes it takes a bit of digging to find what or with whom they're angry. But we can be sure of finding it if we look hard enough.

Ann came in one day crying quietly, complaining she had been depressed for months. It was getting worse every day. She didn't want to do *anything*. She found it difficult to get out of bed in the morning. She spent her days lying on the living-room couch, crying, feeling fatigued for no rea-son, fighting discouragement and defeat. When she couldn't fight anymore, she came to me in tears. Within the hour, she began to mention casually how she missed her home town in Idaho. Maybe that's why she was depressed, she thought. But a wife has no choice to move if her husband decides he wants to change jobs.

She blew her nose and told me how hard it was to give up her job as a secretary back home. She missed her family and friends, and she hadn't been able to make any friends here. As she talked, her expression became more and more grim. It was obvious in that first hour how much anger she still carried toward her husband for "making" her move. But if you can't blame your husband for making you move, what do you do with the anger? You turn it inward and become depressed. And soon your whole family is involved with your depression.

Ann's husband was concerned with her condition. Her children tiptoed around the house trying to stay out of her way because she cried so easily. Her mother flew from Idaho for a week's visit to try to cheer up her daughter. Nothing seemed to help. Her husband felt guilty for having made Ann leave home. He suggested hiring a cleaning lady to help with the housework. The house was clean, but still Ann lay on her bed or couch and blew her nose and felt depressed.

A doctor found nothing wrong physically. He prescribed some tranquilizers and suggested counseling, which sent Ann to me. Once she admitted her anger toward her husband, the battle was half won. Ann could deal with the real problem instead of the smoke screen she'd set up to make herself look like "a good wife" who wanted her husband to do whatever he needed to be happy. Once she admitted she was mad as hell, things began to lift. She stopped punishing her husband in such a subtle way and begin to figure out a solution. They began to negotiate, to discuss, to find compromises, to reach decisions together. In a surprisingly short time, there was no further need for tranquilizers or counseling.

Ann's purpose for the depression was twofold. The first

was to appear sweet and cooperative, rather than angry and resistive. The second was to punish her husband for having chosen to move.

Adler says having insights about purposive behavior is like spitting in your soup. Once you've spit in your soup, you're still free to eat it if you want to, but it doesn't taste as good. Once you find the reason for having a depression, you're still free to stay depressed if you want. But suddenly it seems ridiculous to continue when you can deal with the problem more directly and efficiently.

Sometimes people go into a depression after losing a loved one. Normal grief is one thing, but a prolonged, debilitating depression is another. This type of depression is a silent temper tantrum against *somebody*. Usually there's anger at the deceased person for "having the gall to leave me." Perhaps there's anger at God for having taken the person away. Of course you "can't be mad at God *or* the dear departed," so you turn it inward and become depressed.

If you get a lot of mileage from that depression, like neighbors continuing to give abundant sympathy, along with their casseroles, phone calls from friends and visits from your family, you might stay depressed for months. You're getting too big a payoff for being miserable to give it up. Once you see that, it's easy to make the decision to stop being depressed and get on with the useful side of life instead of the useless, dependent one.

Purposive behavior can also be for good things. If I want a promotion, my behavior will be top efficiency at my job. If I want a boyfriend, my makeup, hairdo and clothes will be impressive, as well as my smile and personality. If I want people to do things for me, my behavior might be helpless. "Clumsy me, I just can't do *anything.*" This brings rescuers rushing to my aid.

Rudolph Dreikurs came up with four goals of misbehavior that are seen in children and adults—attention, power, revenge and assumed disability. We can see them in ourselves if we look at our behavior and feelings with objectivity.

Attention

The first goal of misbehavior is *attention.* As Adler said, our first need is belonging. Sometimes we need attention to show us we belong, and we are significant. We have the need from infancy on. We never outgrow it. As adults we still find ourselves striving to fulfill that need.

How we fill it depends on decisions we made as children about the best ways to get attention. But we all try to fill the need in some way. If I can get enough attention to satisfy me in some healthy, productive way, I won't need to resort to negative behavior to get it. But unfortunately, many of us feel unnoticed in our attempts at usefulness. We get discouraged as days and weeks go by without anyone noticing or commenting on the productive, worthwhile things we do.

But when we do something negative, we get attention all over the place! Maybe we get admonished, scolded, bawled out or punished (even as adults). But we're very aware we've been noticed. And it beats not getting noticed at all.

If I've been a dutiful wife and cooked three nutritious meals a day for weeks, done the laundry, kept the house spic and span and haven't gotten any comments to indicate my efforts are appreciated, I might begin to feel discouraged.

But if I happen to be at a party on a Saturday night and flirt a bit with my next-door neighbor, it feels kind of good to watch my husband rush to my side, bring me drinks and food and give me appraising glances. In fact, I've just learned an important fact of life. I get more attention being "bad" than by being "good." I may begin to let the housework go a bit. I may also begin to flirt more blatantly. After all, if it works, use it, right? If it continues to get results and I now have my husband sticking to me like glue, boy, will I flirt at parties!

My purpose was to get attention, and I got it. I will continue to get it in whatever way works best for me.

Even animals use attention-getting mechanisms. Our dog always chooses to lie down in a doorway or in the middle of a household traffic pattern so we have to step carefully over her. We cannot possibly ignore her that way, as we could if she were being good and quietly lying under a couch someplace. If dogs can figure that out, how can we expect human beings not to make good use of the technique?

Sometimes I see myself doing it. I know I have a need for attention that I will satisfy by hook or crook. Every now and then at meetings or groups, I become aware nobody has noticed me for a while. Everyone else seems to be talking to each other. I'm getting no eye contact from anyone. I begin to feel left out and ignored.

Almost without thinking, I ask a question or make a statement (even if it's dumb) to draw people's attention to me. People look at me and respond to me. I feel "validated," like I'm important after all. I can relax again.

I catch myself doing that from time to time. I feel some amusement because I'd like to think I'm above that sort of thing. I guess none of us is. We all want attention. For that reason we need to be conscious of giving our family, friends and co-workers a reasonable amount of attention so they won't begin to resort to negative behavior to get it.

How do we know if someone is trying to get attention just for the sake of attention or if he or she genuinely needs something? The clue to any behavior goal is our feeling when the behavior is happening.

Parents are familiar with the child who pulls at our pants leg or skirt, saying, "Mommy, can I have a cookie, Mommy, huh, Mommy, can I? Mommy, when is Daddy coming home? Why is it raining, huh? Mommy, Mommy, read me a book. Mommy, play with me." When my children did that routine, I always felt annoyed. The feeling of *annoyance* is my clue to the purpose of their behavior. Once I recognize the fact they're looking for attention, I know I'd better not respond or else I'm teaching them the method works.

It was an entirely different ball game if one of them ran into the house crying, with blood running down a skinned knee. Then there wasn't a shred of annoyance in me. I ran for the soap and water because I knew the need was genuine.

It's amazing how accurate our feelings are in helping us determine the goal of a person's behavior. We always have a choice as to how we're going to respond.

In the case of a whining child, if you give her a cookie she may stop whining for a minute or two. But she'll probably resume the behavior because she wants attention, not food. If she's truly hungry and asking for food, you probably won't feel annoyed because you recognize hunger instead of a bid for attention.

Has your husband or wife ever watched TV for hours on a Sunday afternoon until you began to wish the TV set were broken? I used to get resentful at the weekend time "wasted" when Larry watched football or basketball endlessly (it seemed to me). I found little ways to get his attention, like asking him to open a jar for me or reading him an item from the paper. It didn't matter what. All I wanted was his attention.

If we get enough attention in positive ways, we don't need to use attention getting-behavior to fill our needs.

Power

The second goal of misbehavior is *power.* Sometimes we begin to believe we're worthwhile only if we're in a powerful position. Actually it's not surprising we pick up that behavior. From the time we're born we watch our parents "being powerful" by telling us what to do, what not to do, how to behave and how not to, ad infinitum. It looks to us as though life is a lot more fun for our parents, who "run the show," than it is for us, who are expected to mind.

We form the belief if *we* can be in power we'll be happy. We find friends who are more powerful than we are, and they further inspire us to power. We find friends not as powerful, and we enjoy the heady feeling of power when we're around them. Some of us get hooked for the rest of our lives, trying to "win" in power struggles.

In a power struggle, nobody ever really wins. If I win one power struggle, I lose another. It's only a matter of time. A lot of relationships seem to revolve around continuous power struggles, in which one person wins while the other loses and vice versa.

The clue to recognizing the power goal of misbehavior is when I feel more than just annoyed. I feel angry, threatened, backed against the wall, helpless, frustrated or furious.

When I begin to feel that way, I can recognize my opponent's goal of power. Hopefully I can remember in a power struggle no one wins. The only way to stop one is to remove myself from the struggle.

Remember those little straw Chinese gadgets you used to win at school carnivals? They were designed for two people to put their fingers in and pull against each other. The harder you pulled, the harder it became to remove your finger. The only way to get free was to stop pulling and relax. That's how power struggles work.

The harder I try to beat you, the harder you try to beat me. As long as we continue, we keep the struggle going. If one of us backs out, the struggle ends.

"But I don't want to give in," people say. "It's not fair to let the other guy win all the time."

Refusing to fight is not letting the other guy win. It's simply refusing to participate in that particular activity. If I won't run a race with you, it doesn't mean you win. It just means we haven't raced.

Of course, if you choose to run a race or play a game or engage in a power struggle, you have every right to do so. But if you don't enjoy getting involved in one, you can avoid it by being aware of the purposes—to win, to be powerful, to be strong, to control.

Power does have a place in society. Prison guards need it, and so do bouncers in bars. But it has no good use in personal relationships. Next time you're aware of feelings of anger beginning to rise, think "power struggle." Decide if you want to play the game. If you don't, withdraw from the struggle before it starts or at any point in its progression.

"But how can I get my point across if I don't get mad?" people ask. "It's the only way I can get my kids (or spouse) to listen to me!"

Sometimes that's true. If it is, the relationship needs help. No relationship can continue very happily if it's based on power. There's always a winner and a loser. If you win now, you lose later.

The only way to solve problems is to communicate, and that can be done without power. Ways to do it are discussed in Chapter 6 on communication, beginning on page 97. If we resort to power, we have only a temporary victory until the other guy beats us. And we can be sure he will. It's only a question of when.

Though we usually think of power as being a strong show of aggressiveness, it doesn't have to be. Weakness can be powerful, and it frequently is.

I saw a demonstration in one of my classes that got the message across beautifully. The instructor asked a volunteer to lie on the floor. The rest of us were supposed to pull him to a standing position. We thought it would be easy because there were 30 of us and only one of him. We grabbed arms and legs and shoulders and every part of him we could, and hefted and tugged. As soon as we got him upright and began to let go, he'd slump limply. We had to support him to keep him from falling again.

It didn't take us long to realize even 30 people can't make one person stand on his own two feet if he doesn't want to. Weakness can be more powerful than strength.

The wife who "has headaches" and isn't interested in sex can drive her husband to fury. This is a clear sign of a power struggle he can't win for love nor money. In her very passive way, she's a strong contender for power. All his angry outbursts will do nothing to increase her libido. He can't win. But neither does she because nobody wins in a power struggle.

So why do we have power struggles at all? Simply because we *think* we would be happy if we got our way, if we won or if we were in power. But if we do win through power, we have no mutual respect nor the cooperation that goes with it.

Communication, not power, is the answer.

This is true with our children, too. If we use power to get them to do what we want, we're teaching them the same technique. We can be sure they'll learn quickly and well. If I give my son a sound spanking and send him to his room, I've just taught him that violence solves problems and powerful people win. Why should I be surprised when he hits me or finds ways to embarrass and frustrate me every chance he gets?

Certainly we have the right to tell people what we will do, but we can never "make" anyone do anything. I can say, "I'm not willing to read a bedtime story to you unless your room is straightened up before I come in," then follow through with it. But if I punish my son for not cleaning his room it means I'm into power. He's going to give me a merry chase in trying to achieve it.

Revenge

The third goal of misbehavior is *revenge*. We try to get revenge on people only when we are hurt. Sometimes we take revenge on a person who had nothing to do with our being hurt. At times a person may have so much pain he will strike out to hurt anyone who comes on the scene. When I read of snipers shooting people at random, I can only chalk it up to the goal of revenge. "I'm hurting so I want to hurt somebody back." The victim who gets shot just happened to be handy at the moment.

The way to determine a person's goal is our own response to the behavior. If the goal is revenge, our resulting feeling is hurt. Anytime someone says something to me that hurts my feelings, I can be pretty sure that person wants revenge.

Frequently we use revenge when we've lost in the power struggle and we're hurt. Revenge may be subtle and even sweetly voiced. But it does its job efficiently.

I can think of ways I've used it in my own family. Larry is a thoughtful, loving husband who does almost anything for me. He might buy me gifts, take me to dinner, write me poems and do many romantic things to show me he loves me. I appreciate all those things. But he's never been into house repair, yard work or remodeling. I knew that when I married him. In fact, I chuckled warmly at his statement, "Looking at a hammer gives me a headache." I thought, "Isn't he sweet?" and reread the witty, loving poem he'd just given me.

But over the years I began to feel wistful about "what might have been." I would compare him to my father, who could build anything, fix anything, add rooms, make furniture, whatever. Granted Daddy was never into romance, poetry or wining and dining. I wanted the best of both worlds.

Normally I give Larry a lot of credit for the work he does around the house and yard because I know he's done it just for me and not because he enjoys it. It's strictly a labor of love. I appreciate it more than all the flowers and candy in the world!

But if I'm miffed at him for something, if I feel he's dominated me or treated me unfairly, I can become hurt. Then the goal of revenge rears its ugly head, and I say sweetly over dinner, "Honey, I was at Cheri's house today. She has the most beautiful yard I've ever seen. Don works so hard there you wouldn't believe it. He's wonderful, the way he is constantly doing things around the house and yard. It really shows."

If Larry feels hurt, that's exactly the way he was supposed to feel. I've done my job well and in a very socially acceptable way. I haven't physically attacked him or even yelled and screamed. I have been a sweet, ladylike wife. I even pour him another glass of wine as I smile at him after raving about my friend's hardworking husband. That's revenge!

In any close relationship, we know each other well

enough to be able to hit where it hurts the most. It's because we're the most vulnerable in front of someone we love. That person has more reason to hurt us because we've hurt him or her. We do it to each other in every possible relationship. Parents hurt kids, and kids hurt parents. The closer the relationship, the more we hurt each other. It's because we *are* so vulnerable and because we love each other. It's a shame that where we have love, we also sometimes have revenge, even if it's gift-wrapped in a "nice" comment like the one about Cheri's back yard.

We can avoid close, loving relationships so we will never be hurt. Some people do that. I prefer to love, knowing when I love I risk being hurt. I can stand being hurt even though I don't like it. When I'm able to understand the other person's reasons for needing to hurt, it helps me handle the hurt when it comes.

Frequently we may be the receptacle for someone's goal of hurting. But we may not be the reason. We may be the receptacle because we love each other and can be freer with each other than we are with friends or co-workers.

If I've been put down by an angry client, ignored by a neighbor and cut off in traffic by a rude driver, I may come home with feelings of hurt inflicted by the outside world. Who is the most likely person for me to hurt back? Larry. First because he's handy. Second because we're so close I feel much safer in expressing my feelings toward him rather than to the client, the neighbor or the rude driver.

That doesn't make it *right*. It isn't fair for me to dump on Larry and spare the rest of the world, but sometimes I do. Knowing it makes it easier to bear when I'm unfairly treated because I know another time I'll be the one who treats someone else unfairly.

Assumed Disability

The fourth goal of misbehavior is *assumed disability*. It means giving up. This disability is not organically caused. In its most extreme form, a person with assumed disability is a patient in a mental hospital lying speechless and motionless in a catatonic state. He is unaware of the world around him. He has given up attention-getting mechanisms, power struggles and revenge. He has given up totally. He feels so defeated he chooses, unconsciously perhaps, to give up the ball game altogether.

Fortunately, few of us ever get to that point. But sometimes we give up in lesser ways. An aged person, for example, may get so discouraged with life he gives up and withdraws. He sits in his rocking chair hour after hour, not caring what goes on around him. Nothing we try seems to flag his interest. He gets to the point of not watching TV or reading. He just sits. He doesn't get angry or happy or anxious. He doesn't seem to have any feelings at all. We find ourselves totally at our wits' end. We don't know how to react to him.

That's our clue his goal is assumed disability. When *we* feel like giving up, it's a pretty good indication *he's* given up. We may see it in children or adults of any age, but we don't see it as frequently as we see the other three goals.

Assumed disability is not to be mistaken with a power struggle, in which a person stops doing something just to make us angry. A child who refuses to clean her room may not clean it, no matter what we do. But usually our feelings are frustration, resentment and anger. All these indicate her desire to "win," to be the powerful one. That's certainly different from the assumed-disability goal, in the face of which we feel total confusion and bewilderment, honestly not knowing what to do or where to turn.

Reaction to Behavior

The goals of attention, power and revenge are used constantly and not necessarily in any order. I might be into attention-getting at 10:00 in the morning, into power at 10:05, revenge at 10:15, back to attention at 10:30, and so on all day.

It can be fun trying to figure out your goals. It's even more fun figuring out other people's. Don't *tell* the person what his goal is, even if you think you've just figured it out. To say to your spouse, "Ah-ha! You're into attention getting. I know it!" or "That's a revenge goal if I ever saw one," isn't going to make your relationship ring with peace and harmony. Guess all you want and respond accordingly, but avoid sharing your insights with the person in question.

Just as our feelings are the clues in realizing what someone's goals are, our responses are crucial in the person's decision to continue or stop the behavior. The very best way to make sure any behavior continues is to give it positive attention. The second best way is to give it negative attention.

In other words, if I reward someone with praise, a smile, a hug or a piece of candy, I'm encouraging him to continue what he just did. If I scold, frown, sigh heavily or punish him, I'm still giving him enough payoff for his behavior to make it continue.

We all need to give people the right to their own feelings and behavior, without getting involved in it ourselves. If their behavior imposes on my comfort or my possessions, I have the right to stop it.

"I'm not willing to have my piano scratched by your child's truck. Do you want to take it from him or shall I?"

"I'm watching TV, and your crying is interfering. Do you want to watch quietly with me, or would you rather go cry in your room?"

"When you change clothes three times a day, my laundry really piles up. Would you rather change less frequently, or do you want to do your own laundry?"

In these examples, I'm not willing to be put out by other people's behavior. But neither am I chastising them for it. I'm willing to live and let live. That's one of the most important decisions we can make for our own happiness.

Once we've made that decision, how should we react when someone uses his goals of misbehavior on us?

With the attention-getting goal, if we give attention on demand, we foster bad behavior. We must avoid being manipulated into paying attention at those times. If I feel annoyed by my child's whining and give her attention for it, positive or negative, I'm inviting her to continue whining. I must be unimpressed by the whining and call my friend, turn on the TV set, move the hose or do anything else to keep from responding to the demand, "Pay attention to me!"

However, I must make sure to give positive attention at other times, so my child will know I care.

How do I get out of power struggles? By removing myself. By refusing to continue the game once I realize I'm playing it. It takes two to have a power struggle. If I refuse to get involved, you can't go on alone. It's like trying to ride on a seesaw by yourself.

Revenge is a hard goal not to react to because it hurts. That's what it's intended to do. When I'm hurt it's difficult not to hurt back. But that's what I must do if I'm going to stop the vengeful behavior. If I hurt back, the other person will have more hurt to deal with and an even bigger need for revenge.

Here's where the old saying, "To err is human; to forgive is divine," comes in handy. Try to be divine and forgive rather than hurt back. That stops the cycle. If I can truly forgive a person who has hurt me and continue to love him and accept him in spite of his need for revenge, I can make a significant improvement in our relationship. It helps me a lot to remember, "A misbehaving person is a discouraged he's lashing out and hurting me, I can feel compassion instead of resentment.

If I can find something to *encourage* him about, I'm helping his self-esteem. That will make him less discouraged. He will no longer have a burning need to hurt once he has a better self-image.

Assumed disability is the hardest to deal with. Fortunately, we see it less frequently than the others, so it's not a common problem in our lives. When we try to cope with someone who's given up, we must remind ourselves these people are the most discouraged of all. The only thing we can do to help, in addition to getting professional therapy, is to pour on the encouragement. If we can find one small thing to say in a positive way, we've taken a small step toward building his self-esteem. We measure progress in tiny steps not giant leaps. It can get discouraging for us to try to help a person who's so discouraged he's given up. But it's important to continue trying. We might be the difference between that person's decision to live or die. We certainly affect the quality of his life.

If the person will consent to seeing a counselor, that's terrific. A family counselor who sees the family all together is the most helpful in this case. Everyone involved needs to know the dynamics that have caused the behavior and how to turn the downward spiral upward.

Communicating Successfully

My college speech teacher used to say, "Misunderstanding is common. In fact, understanding is only a happy accident." He may have been exaggerating a bit, but I think our misunderstanding of each other contributes heavily to problems in relationships. The success of every relationship in which I am involved—parent-child, husband-wife, co-worker—depends on communication. Whether that communication is good or bad determines the quality of the relationship.

We use communication skills we learned from our families. Frequently we're puzzled when something we say to a spouse causes him to flare or bristle. To us it seemed a perfectly innocent, perhaps even a complimentary, thing to say. We heard our parents say it a million times. What's wrong with him? In his house that phrase or sentence probably implied some kind of threat. When he hears it now, he reacts as he used to.

The kind of communication I promote is based on the concept of mutual respect. When you and I truly respect each other, we're able to get our messages across with a minimum of misunderstanding or bad feelings. In mutual respect, I respect you and you respect me. In addition, I respect myself, and you respect yourself. If all four of these attitudes are operating, we're off to a good start. If any is missing, we're in trouble.

It's fun to remember a particular encounter with someone and figure out which attitude was operating. If the encounter was genuinely pleasant for both parties, mutual respect was probably involved. If the encounter was unpleasant or threatening, it can be interesting and helpful to realize which of the four attitudes was missing. You can take steps to guard against it in the future.

Thomas Harris explained the concept in his book, *I'm OK, You're OK*. "I'm OK, you're OK" is mutual respect in a nutshell, and it's the best attitude with which to communicate. Sometimes *we* don't feel OK. At other times we think, "I'm OK, *you're* not OK." At still other times we think, "I'm not OK and neither are you." But ideally we should always take the position of "I'm OK, you're OK."

Our Attitudes Affect Our Actions

Occasionally I buy something, and when I get home I regret the purchase and decide to return it to the store. I have four choices in how to go do that. I always chose, "You're OK, I'm not OK." I used to feel like a horrible person if I took anything back to a store. I felt like the salesperson hated me and would reject me for the rest of my life. With that attitude, I reluctantly took the offending object in hand (let's say it was a brown purse) and went back to the store. I skulked miserably to the purse counter, looking as humble and apologetic as humanly possible. I'd smile foolishly and say, "I am *so* sorry to bother you! I bought this purse then realized it was the wrong color. I'd like a refund, but I know that's a lot of trouble for you, and I'm very sorry!" If the saleslady glared and firmly demanded the sales slip, I whipped it out quickly and tried even harder to endear myself to her. My belief was I couldn't stand her disapproval. That whole process was an example of "You're OK, but I'm not. I'm inferior to persons of authority."

Equally untrue is the position of "I'm OK, but you're not." In that case, I would take my new brown purse and walk up to the lady at the purse counter, slam the purse down and demand a refund. My whole attitude would be one of hostility, resentment and disapproval of her, her purses and the whole darn store! I might bark, "I want my money back, and I'll talk to your manager if you give me any trouble." Anything to prove I'm superior and she's inferior.

In the position that *neither* of us is OK, I would probably act similarly to the behavior I just described, but I'd be self-deprecating in addition. "I don't know why I bought this purse in the first place. I hate brown, but I bought it anyway. That shows how dumb I am. I should have known better than to come to this rotten store at all, but I always end up doing the wrong thing." I would need to prove both the saleslady and I are born losers and that goes for our grandmothers, too!

Naturally the best position of all is the one that says

both of us are OK. In that instance, I would feel perfectly free to take the purse back to the counter and say in a pleasant way, "I've changed my mind about this purse, and I'd like a refund please." How simple, and yet how assertive. I would probably get a refund in any of those four positions. But I'd certainly be more comfortable about the whole thing if I came from a position of mutual respect.

Sometimes people say, "But I hate aggressive people. I don't want to be one of those." Neither do I. But aggressiveness is not assertiveness. *Aggressiveness* is the "you're not OK" position. *Assertiveness* is the "I'm OK, you're OK" position, which simply states the problem and/or feelings about it. It's giving you the respect that assumes you're willing to listen to me and help deal with my problem.

Non-assertiveness is the doormat syndrome. If I'm non-assertive, I feel I'm so unworthwhile I'd better just shut up and forget the whole thing. I'll carry this ugly brown purse until I die, but I won't put myself in a position of potential discomfort or disapproval because that's a scary place to be.

When I think I'm not OK, I really feel deep down you're not OK either, even if I act like you are just to win your approval. I can like you only as much as I like myself, so it's really important to believe I am OK. Then—isn't it wonderful?—so are you!

Good Communication

Acceptance is essential to good communication. I don't have to agree with you or approve of your behavior. But if I can accept you however you are, we can have some sort of relationship. With communication and mutual respect, we might eventually be able to understand each other and even come to love each other. But if I refuse to accept you in the first place, our communication won't be much good. I'll be too busy trying to change you, prove I'm right, diminish you or justify my rejection of you. This can only poison our relationship.

Once I accept you, I can begin to guess how it feels to be you. How does it feel to be my father? My boss? My client? My son? My daughter? My husband? I have a little wood plaque that reads, "Oh, Great Spirit, grant that I may never find fault with my neighbor until I have walked the trail of life in his moccasins. (Cherokee Prayer)" If I can get inside your head and *feel* how it is to be you, I can begin to understand your beliefs, fears, reactions and behavior. When I have the sense to put myself in another fellow's shoes, I'm always impressed at how much more easily I can accept him.

One of the most important factors in communication is honesty. Every communications class I teach gets around to asking, "Just how honest should I be?" We can discuss that subject by the hour, and I still struggle for an answer. I personally believe, as I said before, we can have as good a relationship with someone as we are honest with them. While it's not important for me to have close, meaningful relationships with everyone I know (I haven't time; neither do they), I love having close, meaningful relationships with many people. Those are the people with whom I *must* be honest—my husband, my children, my friends.

But the definition of honesty has to include an option of *not* telling everything I know, think or feel. Deep inside

me is a little corner of privacy I reserve only for me. Sometimes I may choose to share it with some people. Sometimes those people are the unexpected ones—perhaps a
stranger I meet on a plane whom I'll never see again. I have
the freedom of deciding what information to share with
whom, but it must be honest. In other words, I don't always
share; but I am always honest in what I *do* share.

Suppose Larry and I are at a party, and in the course of
the evening I find myself attracted to a handsome Latin
bartender named Mando. Is it wise of me to waltz over to
Larry, sip my chablis and say, "Wow, that Mando really
turns me on, you know?" Most men find that information
just a bit threatening, even if they know their wives are not
the roving type.

Actually I am a bit of a flirt, if the truth is to be told.
When I was 13, I always managed to dust the living room
when my big brother's friends were there because I loved
being around the boys. One day my mother warned me I
was entirely too flirtatious for my own good, so I learned to
flirt someplace besides my own living room. To this day I
love to flirt. I enjoy talking to men and feeling kind of
turned on and attractive, but that's where it ends. I shared
that information years ago with Larry—not that I would
have had to because he was capable of noticing it all by
himself. But we've discussed it, he accepts it and continues
to love me. That's the kind of honesty I think is essential.
"Honey, I do dearly love men! Though I may flirt, I love you
most of all. I promise you I will never be unfaithful!"

Once I shared that with Larry, I didn't feel any compul-
sion to share each individual flirtation I indulged in. Suppose I came home from work and said, over the pork chops,

"Boy, I really turned on to Gary this morning. And this afternoon I talked to Steve for a long time. I'm looking forward to my class tonight because Dick will be there, and I think he's terribly attractive. You know who's really sexy? Your new salesman." If I did that, I think Larry's pork chops would begin to taste flat and his enthusiasm might dim. Few of us could listen to a recitation of our mate's turn-ons and not feel some discomfort. But for me to pretend other men leave me cold is dishonest, and I think that would be just as unfair to my husband. I want him to know me really well, to know how I tick and think and feel. But I don't have to tell him every last feeling or thought I experience.

"Honesty with kindness," is one of my mottoes. Hopefully I can give both, but I hope never to be honest with deliberate unkindness.

How Honest Should We Be?

It's difficult to know where our responsibilities lie with friends or people we love and care about. How honest should we be? If Laurie, our 27-year-old daughter, comes home with a new hairdo I think is less becoming to her than the one she had before, should I tell her? If 25-year-old Lisa comes home with a boyfriend I feel dubious about, do I express that opinion?

That's tough. Before I do, I should mention the *purpose* of sharing the information. If I feel my daughter would benefit from having the information, then I'll probably choose to tell her. I'll give her the right to decide for herself what she wants to do with the information. But if I tell my children what I think they should do then get miffed if they don't do it, I'm out of line. This refers to grown-up children. When a child is small, we have the responsibility to set some limits and make some decisions.

In any relationship, I have the right to tell you my feelings or desires if I wish. But I don't have the right to expect you to do anything about them. You may or you may not. If that becomes a problem to me, I have the right to tell you. With good communication, we can negotiate some agreement.

Sometimes we feel simply communicating information to someone should ensure the person follows through. "He knows I want him to paint the fence!" a wife will moan. But knowing it doesn't mean he's going to do it. She has a better chance of getting it painted by telling her husband she'd like it done, but that doesn't mean the job will get done.

How We Communicate Is Important

Seventy-five percent of all communication is non-verbal. What I say is important, but how I look when I say it may be even *more* important. If Lyle comes home from school and announces excitedly he has a part in the school play, he can gauge my enthusiasm level very quickly. If I continue reading my magazine, say "That's nice," and turn the page without looking up at him, my message is one of relative indifference. Though the words I utter may have been the right ones, the rest of my manner showed I was singularly unimpressed.

On the other hand, I might not even say a word and still convey feelings of joy, pride and excitement by putting down my magazine and looking up at him with a face that shines with delight and enthusiasm. I might smile broadly, shake my head in wonder at his accomplishment and give him a big hug. Not a word need be spoken for him to receive my message.

How many times have you used a facial expression to send a message to someone across the room, ranging from "I love you" to "I'm miserable—when can we get out of here?" Usually people in close relationships, like a husband and wife or a parent and child, become experts in sending body-language messages to control, hurt or upset the other person. Sometimes we are totally unaware of doing it.

If my husband is telling me about something that happened at work and notices I look at my watch, wind it, look out the window, inspect my manicure and yawn, he might trail off without finishing the story. If he feels hurt at my lack of interest, he may taste my meatloaf, grab the water glass and drink quickly, set his fork down, stare at the meatloaf, sigh heavily and push away his plate. Not a word was spoken between us, but we've just managed to "tell each other off" in a quiet, non-aggressive way. The battle can continue in subtle ways.

How much better we would be treating each other if we spoke with words, in a respectful, honest way. We could be up front with our feelings, needs, wants and thoughts. Sometimes we kid ourselves by saying, "I don't want to hurt his feelings, so I'd better not tell him this." Then we proceed to let out our resentment and hostility in silent, poisonous ways.

Many times a wife will say, "I want to improve our communication, but how do I get my husband to talk? He comes home every night and grabs a beer and the paper, which he reads till it's time to eat dinner. After dinner he turns on the TV set and falls asleep during the news. I *can't* talk to him. It's like talking to a brick wall. He won't answer, or if he does, it's meaningless . . . like 'uh-huh.' He's totally preoccupied in his own little world."

If it's really that bad, marriage counseling is your best bet. If one party simply refuses to communicate, there's little you can do besides announcing you have a problem and you'd like to talk about it. If he still refuses, *you* suggest a marriage counselor. If there's no response say, "I'm going to call tomorrow and make an appointment. I'd love to have you along, but if you don't want to, I'll go anyway." Though marriage counseling works most easily when both spouses are present, it's amazing how much can be accomplished with only one person there. When you change your behavior, the other person's has to change.

Many times a husband genuinely seems not to understand there really is a problem! He's been told there's a problem, but somehow it's simpler to ignore it and hope it'll go away. If the wife takes responsibility to start doing something constructive about their problems, it is frequently enough incentive to get the husband to go along. Sometimes it works the other way around, when the husband is the one who seeks counseling. In my experience, the person who feels the most hurt is the one who makes the phone call.

Accepting and Self-Disclosing

Perhaps the problem is not serious in your house, and it's simply a matter of *improving* communication. To accomplish that, keep these two steps in mind—accepting and self-disclosing.

If I *accept* you as you are, I'm already on a pretty good

road toward a close relationship. If I *self-disclose,* I share my feelings, thoughts and ideas with you. I don't give you advice, attack you or threaten you.

"I" messages are terrific. "I would just love to go dancing one of these nights," is getting you a lot closer to the dance floor than, "You never take me dancing anymore." A statement that lets you know my feelings is more up front and effective than a manipulative put-down or thinly veiled attack.

Imagine how Larry would feel if I said, "Sally has the neatest husband. He takes her dancing twice a month!" He would feel guilty for not measuring up. Same with, "Remember John, the guy I dated before we started going together? Boy, was *he* a great dancer! We used to have more fun together. We would dance for hours, and I just loved being with him." More up front, but still hurtful, would be the accusation, "I know why you won't take me dancing; you're no good at it. You ought to take dancing lessons, then maybe you'd be willing to go out once in awhile. I guess if I were as rotten a dancer as you I wouldn't want to be caught dead on the dance floor either."

Any time we attack or criticize a person we are using the "I'm OK, you're not OK" position. That violates the ideal of mutual respect. Naturally there are situations that invite criticism, like reviewing movies or proofreading, but right now we're looking at interpersonal relationships.

Using "I" Messages

When we speak in "I" messages there is no violation of respect. We simply state our feelings or beliefs if we do it correctly. Saying, "I think you're really stupid!" is not recommended because that's actually an attack. But "I feel so uncomfortable about having your mother come to live with us," invites more conversation about the subject without attack.

"I'm really down today, and I'm not sure why. But I'm aware of being edgy with everyone."

"I've been wanting to go to a movie lately."

"I'd love a hug."

"I'm worried about how we're going to make the car payments."

These are all good "I" messages that get your point across without criticizing or threatening the listener.

If we need to comment on the other person's behavior, a three-step "I" message helps state the problem in the least threatening way.

1. "When you
2. I feel
3. because . . .

"Eric, when you come home late from school I feel worried because I think maybe something's happened to you."

"Honey, when you smoke in bed I really worry because you might fall asleep with the cigarette in your hand."

"When you kids leave your empty pop bottles in the living room I feel discouraged because I try to keep it neat in there."

"Mother, when you criticize the way I'm raising my children I get upset because I'm doing it the way I think best."

"When you open the mail while I'm talking I feel hurt, like you're not interested in what I'm telling you."

Any of those comments is far less likely to cause trouble than, "Eric, you're a bad boy for coming home late. Go to your room."

"It's rotten enough that you smoke at all, but do you have to do it in bed and burn us all up?"

"I'm sick to death of picking up after you kids. You're all grounded."

"Mother, shut up about the way I raise my kids. You made every mistake in the book."

"You know what you can do with all your mail . . . I'm going to the bar!"

Of course if all our communication were limited to "I" messages, life would get insufferably dull. But it's a good skill for transmitting feelings and problems with the least chance of offending someone.

Listening

Another skill to help foster good feelings with anyone is *listening*. Frequently we're so eager to talk we tolerate the other person's words without actually listening to them. We're already planning what we're going to say as soon as they take a breath instead of hearing what they're telling us.

I love knowing I'm understood. Sometimes that's all I want—just to know Larry understands how I feel. He doesn't have to suggest any solutions or do anything else. The other night I was complaining about how tired I was and how busy and overextended I felt. Larry pointed out it was the lifestyle I'd chosen for myself, and I hated being idle or bored.

That made me feel even more discouraged. Of course, he was right. But no one needed to tell me that. All I wanted was a look of concern and a statement like, "Wow, you really *have* been busy, haven't you?" or "Sounds like you're working hard" or "I'll bet you *are* tired." Any of those would have assured me he understood, and I would have felt loved.

Too many times we think we must jump in and give solutions to somebody's problem when all they want is for us to understand them. If Lindsay is complaining his term paper is due tomorrow and he hasn't started it yet, I'm going to improve our relationship if I say something like, "Oh, wow, I'd be discouraged too if I were you," rather than, "Well, you knew it was due tomorrow. When will you ever learn to start a few days earlier?"

Anything that smacks of superiority in an exchange is bound to leave the other person feeling inferior and uncomfortable. I have never heard anyone put me down and thought or said, "Thank you so much for pointing out my weaknesses and flaws. It inspires me to do better next time!" All it may inspire me to do is get one up on him the next time.

A very effective tool we've acquired at our house is "on a scale of 1 to 10." It's useful to pinpoint feelings for greater understanding so better decisions can be made. We use it for something as simple as what movie to go to. One of us might say, "On a scale of 1 to 10, I'd like to see *Rocky*, a 9."

"I'd give it a 7," the other might answer. "How about *Kramer vs. Kramer?*"

"Oh, a 5."

"I'd say a 7 on that one, too. Okay, if you have a 9 on *Rocky*, I'm willing to see that one because I'm 7 either way."

Sometimes we think the other person knows how we

feel, yet they may have no concept of how deeply we feel it. Larry has an inordinate penchant for Disneyland. Every year as we approach vacation time, he scores it a 10. Actually, on a scale of 1 to 10, he would give it a 20! Having been there about 30 times, I've plunged it down to a 0 on my priority scale. But I recognize how much joy it gives Larry, and I want him to enjoy it. There's no reason we have to agree on some things. Now when we go to California, Larry visits the Magic Kingdom while I stay with friends.

We use the 1-to-10 scale for many decisions—how we feel about having the pine tree chopped down, where we go to dinner, whether we invite the Christensens over for cards. We use it for almost anything we need to decide when two or more different opinions are involved in making the decision.

Closed Responses and Open Responses

To be good communicators, we should know the difference between closed responses and open responses. A *closed response* leaves nothing for the other person to say. An *open response* invites a further response. If Lisa says, "Betsy and I had a big argument last night," I can stop the flow of conversation very quickly with this closed response, "Oh, you and Betsy are always arguing about something. Set the table." The impression I give is I'm not interested in what she has to say.

An open response might be, "Oh, what was it about?" or anything that lets her know I'm interested. "Tell me about it" or "How did it come out?" or "How do you feel about it?" or "What are you going to do now?"

You may know people who always seem to talk in

closed responses. Everything they say has a ring of authority about it and is said with such finality one wouldn't consider questioning it, at least not out loud. These are people I find myself skipping over when I'm looking for a lunch partner. Instead I seek someone who seems to enjoy giving and taking. They like to talk, and they like to listen. Just for fun, listen to yourself in your next conversation. Notice whether you have more closed responses or open responses. I'm sure it will vary with each person you meet, but the more open responses you use, the better communication you invite.

Sometimes we need to remind ourselves no matter how effectively we communicate, we won't always agree, see eye to eye or understand the other person and his views.

My brother, Paul, and I are delighted with every opportunity we get to communicate. We can discuss any issue for hours on end, sometimes to the boredom of anyone unfortunate enough to be around us for any length of time. We will happen on a subject like religion, the Equal Rights Amendment or legalized marijuana and investigate every possible facet we can think of. We always take opposite sides just for the fun of lively communication. Neither of us gets angry or feels threatened. Neither of us has to win. That's probably the key to our enjoyment and our continued special relationship. He has opposite views from mine on a lot of subjects, but I love him dearly and feel no need for any one-upmanship. So communication can be simply a delightful pastime, with no need to convince.

It's because of *acceptance*. If I truly accept Paul as he is, I don't need to convince him of my views. There's no need or cause for anger and hurt. It simply doesn't matter.

Sometimes it's good for us to heed the advice of Alfred Adler. "Let others be right half the time, even though you know they're wrong."

Giving and Receiving Gifts

I can't finish this chapter on communication without mentioning gifts and presents. I'm convinced gifts cause more unhappiness than many more obvious sources of unhappiness. That's partly because a "should" is usually involved in a gift. If I'm the giver, I probably feel I "should" give some kind of gift for an occasion. With very few exceptions, that causes a problem. Trying to find the perfect gift is a losing battle but one we struggle with frequently.

The process is relatively simple if the recipient is not someone close to us, like one of our children's teachers. We can give a candle or a plant and feel good about it. A wedding gift for a friend's son poses no great problem because there are plenty of good, reliable wedding gifts.

The anguish comes when we need a gift for someone dear to us. We feel we ought to know just what would make that person happy. The closer they are, the harder it becomes. I have spent long hours browsing through Christmas catalogs. I've spent more hours tramping from store to store looking for the right gifts to make my husband's or children's faces light with joy when they open the package.

And do they? Usually not. I remember one Christmas when Lyle was about 13. I had spent the usual hundreds of hours thinking about, buying and wrapping gifts. When I came to the last stretch, the Christmas stockings, I decided to include a bottle of shaving lotion shaped like a stack of

poker chips because I thought it would make Lyle feel
grown up.

When I woke up Christmas morning, I was met at the
bedroom door by a grim Lyle. He announced he hated the
shaving lotion. I burst into tears! After all the time and
energy I'd spent in trying to anticipate what might please
him, I knew I'd failed. Lyle was chagrined and apologetic.
He immediately applied copious amounts of shaving lotion to prove how much he loved it, but the damage had
been done.

Though I was the giver that time, I have been the
disappointed recipient more times than I care to remember.
My heart goes out to people on whichever end of the stick
they find themselves. It's a no-win situation because there is
no solution. If I sound negative, I have a whole collection
of stories from disappointed clients and friends to back up
my theory.

A couple of birthdays ago, Larry gave me an expensive
pair of scissors he thought I'd love. I'd lost a similar pair
years ago. But what I really longed for was a wrought-iron
chair for the patio. I had long since replaced the scissors. I
pretended to like them for the rest of the day, but the next
day I asked if I could get a refund at the scissors store. He
was very hurt and disappointed. He stood by grimly while I
made the transaction, then we continued on our way to visit
my father in another city.

What might have been a lovely trip was a pretty miserable one. Both of us were hurt and angered by each other's
defense. We pleaded our cases for 200 miles. Finally we
understood each other's views better than we had for the 25
years we'd "gift-ed" each other. I realized as a child, I got to

ask for what I wanted. Mama would ask well before our birthdays what we'd like that year, and I always chose a doll. A very *particular* doll. No other doll. Part of the fun of birthdays or Christmas was choosing what we wanted more than anything else.

Larry had an entirely different view of birthdays. They should be full of surprises. His parents didn't ask what the children wanted. Instead they surprised them. Larry must have liked it because to this day he loves to be surprised and to surprise.

Once we established these facts and realized the difference in our expectations, we were able to come to some kind of peace with ourselves. He knows I don't like surprises, and he lets me choose whatever I want. I am so happy you wouldn't believe it!

He shakes his head in wonder when I point out *those* earrings in the window that I want for my birthday. He buys them for me, and I open them with great glee on the big day. He can't understand my delight over something I already know about. On the other hand, I make sure to surprise him with something totally unexpected, and he always likes it! It's simple when we come right down to it. The only reason it took so long to figure out is because of our "shoulds" about gift-giving.

I believe we can solve the gift problem by taking some time to talk about each other's likes and preferences. Give the gift *he* wants, not the gift *I* want to give. If the recipient chooses to exchange the gift, try not to feel hurt. It's humanly impossible to provide the perfect gift most of the time, anyway.

Establishing Priorities

Once I learned about priorities, life became understandable. It's easier for me to put up with people's peculiarities after I identify their priorities and see how they clash with mine. Basically there are four priorities—*superiority* (or significance), *comfort, pleasing* and *control*. There are no right or wrong, better or worse priorities—just different ones. But we each rate them differently according to our beliefs, attitudes and needs. For each of us they're vitally important.

Most of us can figure out how we rate each priority once we understand how they work.

Superiority

The first priority is *superiority* or *significance*. If I rate that one high, I have a need to be superior. I feel if I am *not* superior, I'm not worthwhile at all. It doesn't mean I try to be superior to other people. It means I need to do a superior job in whatever I'm undertaking.

If I'm into superiority and I want to see my friends, there is no way I'm going to invite them over for cheese sandwiches. I've got to have a gourmet dinner served on perfectly matched china and crystal. That's why many invitations go unextended. People want to entertain but aren't willing to compromise their standards.

If I'm into superiority I avoid meaninglessness. I have to be busy, productive and achieving, never waste time or do anything insignificant. If I sit, I must be reading or mending. If I talk on the phone, I must make a shopping list at the same time. I exercise during TV commercials. If I'm a ditch digger by trade, I will dig the best ditch it is possible to dig.

There is nothing wrong with superiority. In fact, it helps us achieve great things. But people who are into superiority pay the price of overinvolvement, fatigue, stress and an overload of responsibility. If we see the quest for superiority taking over our lives, we might want to make a conscious effort to lower our standards. I can rate superiority as my top priority yet refuse to indulge in it every waking moment. I can deliberately serve cheese sandwiches to show I am not going to be 100% superior.

There is another kind of superiority that we sometimes see as humility or goodness—moral superiority. If that's my goal, I need to prove constantly to the world how generous, patient, long-suffering, martyrish, good and moral I am. If I'm at a party and the buffet line forms, I make it a point to be the last in line. I invariably hold the door open for everyone and give the most money to the church benefit. I'll work like a dog for my family and never allow myself any fun. The message is always, "See how good I am?"

There are probably hundreds of kinds of superiority we might indulge ourselves in. Fortunately for us, we can't exercise them all. I have a friend whose superiority rests in her home. She has the most beautiful home she can. It's as nearly perfect as possible already, but Marjorie continues to improve it, redecorate it, clean it and apologize for "the mess." She can take other things in her stride, but the house is the measuring stick for her superiority.

Another friend puts her efforts into being the most beautiful. The bulk of her budget goes to her hairdresser, closely followed by her facial lady, the cosmetics department at Goldwaters and by enormous expenditures on new clothes from "the better stores." It doesn't matter that her floors look like the Gobi Desert. The important thing to her is she is impeccable and appropriately dressed and coiffed.

I might be superior at being the most nutrition-minded mother on the block. No junk food for my kids! My children are stuffed with bran, alfalfa sprouts and carrot shakes. I'd get a lot of mileage out of letting everyone know I subscribe to *Prevention* and my entire family munches protein tablets like other people eat popcorn.

Or I might be into exercise. While other families relax around the TV set, mine would be jogging, biking, taking swimming lessons and competing in swim meets, Little League and hiking clubs. My claim to fame would be physical fitness, and my running suit would be my badge of superiority.

Education is another common proving ground. Sending our children to private schools rather than public, making sure they do their homework and urging them to try harder so they can get into the better colleges and get multiple degrees shows the world we must be superior to have such superior children.

Music. Arts. Sports. There are thousands of ways to be superior. There is even an unexpected one! "If I can't be the best, I'll be the best at being *the worst!*" The juvenile delinquent frequently chooses that way to be superior, and he works hard at proving he's rotten. Organized crime is filled with highly successful, superior people.

Alfred Adler believed man is born feeling inferior and spends the rest of his life striving for superiority. It's not surprising we've discovered so many ways to accomplish that goal.

Comfort

Another priority is *comfort—creature comfort.* Comfort is so precious to me even I can't believe it. Once I became aware of the comfort priority and how much I work to achieve it, I keep seeing ways I plan my life around comfort.

I loathe being uncomfortable. I don't want to be too hot, too cold, hungry, thirsty or tired. This means I put a lot of thought into making sure I am perpetually fed, quenched, rested and at a perfect 98.6F body temperature. These are not easy tasks.

I became aware of how peculiar my standards were at our homecoming parade one year in Flagstaff. Homecoming is held in October, and Flagstaff tends to be on the nippy side. I arrived on the scene of the parade prepared with a light jacket to ward off the chill. (After a good breakfast, of course.) In a little while I felt warm, so I took off the jacket. But in a few minutes the wind came up, so I put it back on. Then it seemed hot again.

Pretty soon I began to feel embarrassed because I was in a continual process of donning or shedding the jacket. Everyone around me either wore one or they didn't. They seemed perfectly content, but my private thermostat kept sending my brain vague uncomfortable messages. Finally I was determined to be as strong as the other people, so I kept my jacket off and shivered grimly for the remainder of the parade.

I am the butt of much laughter from my family because of my comfort priority. And I've learned to laugh with them. But nothing will swerve me from seeking comfort. I sometimes drive three blocks out of my way to turn right onto a busy street rather than facing the uncomfortable tension of making a left turn. Lately I've been making myself "stand it" for personal growth, but I long for the days when I let myself do it.

People who love comfort hate stress and will do anything to avoid it. If they're also after superiority, two priorities butt heads. The stronger one wins. I've realized my need to be superior is the only thing that keeps me from taking to my nice firm bed with a heating pad and a bag of peanut clusters and spending the rest of my life there. (I might replace the heating pad with a fan in summer.) It's a good thing I love to play the piano for sing-alongs and give speeches and teach classes because I sacrifice my comfort to achieve those jobs.

Nonetheless, comfort ranks high. Comfort people hate to wait for anything. Instant gratification is what we want and lots of pleasure. We love sleep and food. There is no way on earth I would ever consent to going camping and sleeping on the ground in a sleeping bag. I would go into the wilds only in a luxuriously equipped van complete with air conditioning and a giant refrigerator. The price a comfort person pays is usually diminished productivity. We'd rather not get off our duffs.

Pleasing

Another priority is *pleasing*. Pleasers must urgently avoid rejection. People who like to please are usually nice to be around because they are sensitive to your every wish and frequently try to fill them for you. They're friendly, considerate, generous, non-confrontive, empathetic, flexible and undemanding. The fact my husband is a pleaser makes a beautiful combination for us because he often gives in to my desires for comfort.

Recently, when we spent the night in a hotel room with twin beds, we found his was nice and firm and mine was soft and lumpy. Naturally I was distraught and filled with panic at the thought of a sleepless night on that miserable mattress. Larry, dear, dear Larry, in his zest to please, suggested we trade beds. I will be forever grateful. If you're into comfort, be sure to marry someone who is into pleasing.

The only trouble comes when Larry needs to please other people, sometimes at my expense. For instance, if we go out for coffee after a movie, I begin looking at my watch about 10:30, aware if I don't get to bed I might be tired the next day. Though I'm inching out of the booth, Larry is charming the socks off the waitress, asking how she enjoys working there, where she's from and how was it there in Oklahoma City. The waitress is delighted with all the attention, but I'm losing 5 minutes of my precious sleep!

Because we've learned about priorities, we're able to laugh at these situations. I willingly allow him 5 more minutes with the lady at the cash register, and he cuts short his conversation out of deference to me.

Pleasing works well in conjunction with the "moral superiority" goal, in which one can always be kind, giving and thoughtful, thus proving how moral one is. Fortunately, no one is ever a 100% pleaser. Everyone has a stopping point, at which he will stand up for his rights, sometimes quite aggressively. People who have tried to gain acceptance and approval by pleasing usually have a lot of resentment stored up. When the resentment rears its ugly head, these people become inordinately furious. They tend to give in *too* much and feel self-pity because of it.

Control

The last priority is *control,* including control of self and control of others. A controller believes he is truly worthwhile only when he is in control of a situation. He must urgently avoid humiliation, ridicule, taking risks or losing control in any way. The price he usually pays for that state is some distance from other people, reduced spontaneity and reduced creativity. He is too busy controlling to allow for much freedom or flexibility in his life.

Controllers make superb leaders. We might assume most presidents of giant corporations are excellent at control. Controllers are organized, reliable, productive, practi-

cal, law-abiding, persistent, responsible, ambitious, indus-
trious, precise and steadfast. Mothers and fathers frequently
fall into the controlling seat when their children are young.
It's sometimes difficult to let that seat go as they get older.

Controllers may be bossy and overly concerned with
order. They want to win at all costs. They may see others as
inconsiderate and may be full of demands.

Lily Tomlin, in her delightful "Edith Ann" role, described the controller well. "People say I'm bossy," admitted
Edith Ann from her giant rocking chair. "I'm not bossy. I
just have better ideas."

Those of us who like to control believe we are here to
save the world. If everyone would just listen to us, their lives
would be straightened out in no time. Though frequently
controllers are aggressive, they may also be found among
the "weak." A weak position is sometimes the strongest of
all. A depressed person can rule the entire household from
his gloomy bed. There is no question of who is in control.

Power struggles are frequent between controllers, as
each party firmly believes his position is the right one.
Many times in marriage counseling we find the problems
discussed are not the real problems at all but symptoms of
power struggles between two controllers.

One delightful couple I worked with had a great series
of complaints about each other that included things like,
"He even tells me how to clean house." "She vacuums first,
then dusts. I tell her she should dust first *then* vacuum,"
he explains.

Where you and I might find some humor in the big
deal this couple has made out of trivialities, it isn't funny to
them. It doesn't take an expert to see the issue is not dust

but something bigger. Both people are into control, and each gets upset over any issue that violates his need to control. The same couple fought over the proper way to empty ice-cube trays. Ice cubes, dust or money—the important thing is, "I know what is best. You'd better do things my way, or I'll get angry/upset/whatever makes people cooperate with me."

I wince slightly at the memory of myself a few years ago saying in martyred tones, "If only people in this house would just cooperate with me!" To which Larry couldn't resist replying, "You mean you want them to do whatever you say." I didn't think it was cute at the time, but in retrospect I recognize he was absolutely right.

I admit I have a lot of controlling priority in my makeup, and nothing would please me more than telling everyone in the whole world what to do and having them do it. But I've learned over the years it doesn't work, so I have to control my controlling. I've had to learn to live and let live, as much as I can stand to. Now and then I allow myself a teeny-weeny bit of advice to my children, husband or whoever will listen, like, "Sure does look like snow out there. I think *I'll* take a coat!" But when they totally ignore my good advice and leave the house in their shirt sleeves, I'm able to gulp and know I've learned to let go of my controlling, almost.

A Clash of Priorities

When we find ourselves uncomfortable, we can usually find two of our priorities butting heads. For instance, my oldest and dearest friend wrote me a letter saying her son had decided to attend the University of Arizona in Tucson. She asked me to consider letting him live with us because there was such a shortage of housing on campus. She said he would help around the house and pay room and board, too, and she'd feel good knowing he was with us. She asked me to please let them know as soon as possible.

Instantly I felt discomfort. I could trace it pretty quickly to two of my priorities in conflict—pleasing and comfort. I would love to please my old friend and welcome her son, but my comfort priority was highly threatened by another person moving in. Although I wish I were the type who opens her home to one and all (the more the merrier), I am not. I love privacy. I love being able to show up at break-fast in my old faded flannel nightgown and look glum if I want to. With "company" I'd feel I had to wear a robe and look pleasant.

It took me a couple of hours to make my decision. Comfort won. I wrote my old friend I would meet her son at the airport and have him stay for a few days until he could find a place. But I wasn't willing to have him live here.

In double binds you have to choose one priority or the other, but you can't have them both. This is where so much of our discomfort comes from—trying to choose. For in-stance, if Lyle says, "Mom, can I have a birthday party?" my priorities start to struggle. The superior mother would say, "Of course, sweetie pie, invite 40 of your best friends." So would the pleasing mother. But the mother who values comfort would be turning gray and looking toward the heavens for help. Because I value all three, I would have to do some serious thinking.

I might discard superiority first and indulge in pleasing by agreeing to a party. But I'd also be kind to my comfort priority by setting some limits. "Sure, kid. How about six friends, and I'll give you money for hamburgers and a movie?"

If he hasn't had a birthday party in 10 years and has just gotten over an attack of mononucleosis during which I realized how much I love him, I might even decide to forego the comfort almost entirely and let him have 20 friends and a barbeque in the back yard. I would be making a conscious decision to please him and give up my comfort for a few hours. There is no earthly way I can have them both.

Dispelling Myths

We all grow up believing myths. Some are handed down to us lovingly by our parents or grandparents. Some we learn from friends, books or teachers. Some we figure out all by ourselves. But however we got those beliefs, they are dead wrong.

Let me tell you some of the mistaken beliefs I picked up along the way and eventually discarded when I realized they were not valid.

People Can Make Me Mad or Hurt My Feelings

Baloney. It used to be nice when I could blame someone else for my bad feelings, but I know *I* am the only one responsible for my feelings. I can choose to be happy, sad, anxious, worried, calm or anything I want. I'm capable of controlling the thoughts that control my feelings. *You* can't make me angry. Only *I* can make me angry. Sometimes its difficult to remember that. But I know I'm the person in charge of my feelings. I will feel nothing I don't want to feel.

I didn't believe it when I first heard it. When Dr. Oscar Christensen was doing a demonstration of family counseling for one of our classes, I felt myself bristling at one of the teenage girls who was obviously trying to goad him into anger. He never responded with anger. After class I said to him, "You *were* really angry inside, weren't you?"

"No," he said.

"How could you help not being angry?" I demanded incredulously.

"I saw what she was trying to do," he answered, "and I wasn't going to take the hook. It was easy for me not to become angry when I saw what her goal was."

I walked away feeling skeptical, but now I believe him. Most of the time I can also do it. It sometimes becomes a game to identify the person's goal and analyze my choices. Then I decide on my plan of action or how I choose to respond and think and feel.

I rarely get angry anymore. But I know I can if I want to. I also know whose fault (choice) it will be.

I Can't Help My Feelings

Oh yes, I can. I can wallow in grief if I want to. I can be filled with agonized anxiety if I choose. Or I can be content. It's all up to me. All I need to do to change my feelings is to change my belief, my attitude or my thoughts.

There Are Some Things I Cannot Forgive

Oh, really? Does that mean in my infinite superiority I have the right to stand in judgement and decide who will and who will not be forgiven? Who handed me that authority? On what golden stone is it chiseled I know all and can say, "This is infinitely right and that is infinitely wrong?"

I used to believe I had the knowledge, wisdom and right to judge and blame forevermore, if I so decreed it. But life is certainly more pleasant since I've decided to forgive anyone for anything. It didn't do any good *not* to forgive. I like the feeling of lightness I get when I decide to forgive. It's interesting they taught us that concept in church, Sunday school and synagogues when we were little kids, but they never told us it was sound mental health. Maybe I would have forgiven more people earlier if I'd understood it would make *me* feel happier.

I Must Not Make Mistakes

It's impossible not to make mistakes unless we just take to our beds for the rest of our lives, which would be a pretty big mistake in itself. The only horrible mistake might be one from which we didn't learn. I love the old saying, "Don't say *if only,* say *next time.*"

My favorite saying, "Have the courage to be imperfect," allows me to make mistakes and helps me accept them. When I allow myself to make some mistakes, I'm less inclined to get upset over others' mistakes.

I urge parents to teach their children imperfection is OK and perfection is *impossible*. We are the strongest models our children ever have. If my children can see me take a sheet of burned cookies out of the oven and not go completely to pieces, they learn Mom makes mistakes and she accepts them. Life goes on. Not that I encourage sloppiness, forgetfulness or irresponsibility. My children see me fulfill my obligations and follow through on the things for which people depend on me. But when I make a human error, I'm not devastated and filled with self-loathing.

It's Wrong to Love Myself

Remember the poster that read, "God doesn't make junk?" I believe it. Humility was such a virtue in my family it was a new concept for me to be encouraged to love myself. But love myself I do! And it's neat. Even the Bible teaches us to love our neighbors as ourselves. If I don't love myself very much, I can't love them very much either. I have a real obligation to society to love myself as much as I can. Then I will be able to love *you* as much as I can.

Don't Take Risks

Another favorite poster is one that reads, "A ship in the harbor is safe, but that's not what ships were built for." I love that thought. Picturing a ship crouching safely in the harbor is almost pathetic to me. I have a dubious habit of attaching human feelings to inanimate objects. When I do that with a ship, I feel sure it would be happy only when it's sailing! I know it would experience danger sometimes. But it'd be happy and excited exploring the seas, experiencing the wind and braving the storms, not to mention the pleasure of encountering new people and adventures. When we begin shutting out too many of life's risks, we begin shutting out life itself.

I don't recommend taking risks just for risk's sake. I have no desire to drive my car over the Grand Canyon or to go hang gliding. But if there is something I want to experience, attain or achieve, I strongly consider making the effort, even though I know there may be risks involved.

Having been an overprotected child while growing up, I was an overprotective mother for years. My children occasionally chide me for it. As Laurie says, "I don't resent it, but I regret it." At 27, she's married to Pete, who is encouraging her to take some risks. She recently mentioned Pete has some scars on his body, and she doesn't.

"Pete says it's the only body he has, and he wants to get all the use he can out of it," she said. "I realized I had grown up thinking this is the only body I have, so I've got to take good care of it. But I want to think more like Pete does." Pete makes sense.

Not that I think we should *not* take care of our bodies. On the contrary, I'm a believer in vitamins, exercise and diet. But those are things to keep my body functioning in top shape so I can use it to enjoy life, go places, see things and open up to new experiences. And I can't do that without taking some risks.

I Must Keep Striving for Perfection

If a thing is worth doing, it's worth doing *imperfectly.* As I said before, there may be small exceptions like brain surgery that demand perfection, but not life's trivialities. Housecleaning and cooking do not require perfection. I've decided it's better to have a patio party for my friends and serve hamburgers on paper plates than to think I should serve Beef Wellington on fine china and never have the party at all.

Life Is Serious Business

Sometimes life *is* serious business. But I think most of the time we can be more lighthearted than we are. We *make* life a serious business when we could just chuckle. My friend Bill McCartin comes to mind with his saying, "We take ourselves so seriously!" He said it with a smile, shaking his head at the big deal we make of trivialities. When I'm able to remember that statement, and the way he looked when he said it, I feel an immediate release of tension. Usually I smile at myself.

Sometimes I suggest to irate families if they saw their situation on a TV comedy show, they'd think it was hilarious. They can usually conjure up a reluctant grin at the mental picture. We *live* situation comedies. The more we can maintain a sense of humor about life, the less we're bothered by problems.

When I'm Right, I've Got to Prove It

The first time I heard the concept, "Take the right and

wrong out of it," was at Recovery, a self-help group I refer people to now and then. I had a hard time buying the message, but gradually it began to make sense to me. So many times we go for a symbolic victory in our discussions or behavior with people because we *have to be right!* Once we make the decision to quit judging and cut out those symbolic victories, life gets immeasurably easier.

First of all, it's really difficult to know for sure we *are* right. Admittedly, I think I am most of the time, but so does Larry. How can we both be right? Actually we both *are* from our own viewpoints. But if we both want to prove our rightness to each other, we find ourselves in continual power struggles.

When I decide I'd rather enjoy life than be superior, I can relax. As one of our friends says, "I'd rather be happy than right." It boils down to a conscious letting go of the need to be superior. Once I'm willing to do that, it's easy for me to say, "You may be right" or "I can see you feel that way" or "Interesting!"

I still have the right to feel or believe any way I choose. But I no longer need to try to get you to agree with me. I'm willing to live and let live, and I am much more content.

Happiness Is the Feeling I Want to Have

One poster I like reads, "Happiness is a decision not a destination." Abraham Lincoln gets credit for saying, "People are about as happy as they make up their minds to be." I agree! One of my clients sighed heavily and said, "I thought if I got a third college degree, I'd be happy. Now I've got my Ph.D., and I'm still miserable."

He's coming for counseling because he realized he

won't become happy by achieving. Then how can he be happy? He can do it by making the decision to be.

I can be as happy or as unhappy as I choose to be. It's easier for me to be happy living in Tucson than I would be living on a farm in Australia. I prefer cities, and I love Tucson. But if I *had* to live on a farm in Australia, I would have my choice of living there happily or unhappily. I have that choice at all times.

The other day I made a 9:00 a.m. appointment with a client who could only come early in the morning. *I* call 9 a.m. early because I like to read the paper with breakfast, get my housework done, then get dressed and go to the office. I prefer starting appointments at 11 a.m.

But I made a grand concession that day and dutifully set my alarm for 7:30. I reluctantly got up, gulped my breakfast while I scanned only half the paper, threw in a load of laundry, got dressed and left the bed unmade. I raced, breathless and wild-eyed, into my empty office where I waited and waited and waited. After 20 minutes I called the answering service to see if there were any messages. "Yes," said Sue. "Your 9:00 canceled. I was to call you at home, but I forgot. I'm sorry."

I sighed heavily, hung up the phone and thought of my half-read paper, my clothes in the washer and the unmade bed. I felt my anger rising.

Then I realized my choices. I could be upset if I wanted to, or I could be happy. It took no more than 3 seconds to know which was more pleasant—being happy. So I picked up a book I'd read and loved, and I settled down in my nice comfortable chair for an hour of quiet reading. I can honestly say it was a happy hour. I *always* have that choice.

Sometimes I choose to be unhappy, but I know it's my decision. Happiness is not a feeling at all but a decision we can make any time we want.

We Need to Depend on Each Other

I have lived two lives. For 35 years I depended on people. Totally. Ad nauseum. I went from depending on my parents to depending on my husband, with a lot of friends I depended on along the way. As a dependent person, I would have gotten a blue ribbon. I was a champ. But I was always being disappointed.

In the years since then, I have become quite independent. I love my husband, but I'm happy whether he is at home or out of town. I'm delighted to see my children when they come around, but I'm also happy counseling, writing, playing the piano, shopping, sewing, keeping house or being with friends. I am no longer a dependent person.

I remember the night I came home from a class and announced proudly to Larry, "Guess what! I realized today I don't *need* you anymore! Now I'm staying married to you because I *want* you instead of needing you!" To say Larry was threatened is an understatement. He was devastated. He was upset, unsettled and furious. What did I mean, I didn't need him? What was marriage for?

He saw that as the beginning of the end, but now, 10 years later, he agrees independence is the greatest thing that's happened in our marriage. We're free to love each other and enjoy each other, but we no longer see each other as responsible for our happiness.

Any time we're disappointed, we've been leaning on

someone. If I lean on you and you move, I'll fall. It's that simple. How much more comfortable it is to stand on my own two feet and know I *won't* fall! It's still fun to act dependent sometimes, if I know it will work, like when I found a big black bug in my office. I ran, arms flailing, for the waiting room and announced my plight to a handsome client. He ran to my aid and killed the bug. What would I have done if I'd been the only one in the office? I'd have killed the bug, of course.

I know I can be independent if I have to, but sometimes I still enjoy being a little dependent because it's easier. The main thing to keep in mind is that it *is* a choice. I'm warm in the knowledge I can be very self-reliant when I want to be.

It's still perfectly permissible to ask for help or give help. It's desirable to give help when it's needed. But how wonderful it feels to know I can take care of myself. I can enjoy family and friends because I like them, not because I need them. I think that's a far greater compliment. They know I don't need them. They know I enjoy them, but I'm also happy when they're not around. I would hate to be a mother whose children feel terrible when she's alone. I much prefer their knowing I'm happy alone or with people.

Competition Brings Out the Best in Us

This is a subject I've argued with great animation with friends. I've come to realize I'm one of the few people I know who doesn't believe it. Competition is the American Way. We pay good money to watch people compete in sports. We watch people compete in game shows on TV. We encourage our children to compete in spelling bees, swim meets or beauty contests.

Alfred Adler said we can have either competition or cooperation but never both. Why would we want to choose competition over cooperation? The price we pay is not worth it.

Here's an example. I want to be a successful counselor, and I give it my best. But the day I start competing with other counselors is the day I begin to be unhappy. I would be constantly measuring. Who had more clients today, Beth or I? Did she make more money than I did? I would be preoccupied with comparing and deciding which of us is more successful. If I'm ahead today, I risk failing and watching her surpass me. I would be constantly on edge—ahead, behind, triumphant, chagrined. My state of mind would be dependent on where I stand in The Race.

On the other hand, if I'm cooperating instead of competing, I can be free to enjoy my work all the time. I won't know whether I'm ahead or behind because I'm not making it my business to find out. I'll be happy knowing I'm doing the best I can. The other counselors can do as they please.

Only when I compete do I have anything to lose. Why would I want to add that concern to my life? I would go so far as to say, "Competition brings out the *worst* in us."

I Need (Whatever)

I probably don't. I probably just want it. We don't have too many needs, but we have a great many wants. That's OK, but we mustn't mistake them for needs. Somehow saying we need something gives us permission to demand it and get upset if we don't get it. "I need sex every night," my client Don says, "and Marcia won't give it to me." Getting Don to admit he *wants* sex every night but would certainly survive if he never got any at all took some doing. But he finally agreed. Then he and Marcia could begin to negotiate as to how often they'll have sex.

Marcia, on the other hand, says, "I need to go out more often, and he always wants to stay home." She would enjoy going out, but she doesn't need it. Maybe they should trade some going out for some sex, but it's certain neither person *needs* either activity. They just *want* it. Although it may not seem important, language is a strong influence in determining our feelings. The more we can reject "helpless language" the more able we are to cope with our problems.

I Can't Stand (Whatever)

I've talked about this before. Albert Ellis says, "There is nothing you can't stand. You don't have to like it, but you can stand it." We need to get that phrase out of our vocabularies and substitute, "I don't like . . . " or "I'm uncomfortable with . . . " or "I prefer not to . . . " We need to know we *can* stand just about anything. Knowing it makes us stronger.

I Need People's Approval

We don't need approval. We can stand disapproval very well. We just don't like it.

But let's say we *want* approval, which most of us do. One friend admits he'd go through fire for a pat on the back. Many of us would have to admit the same trait. It would be lovely to have everyone approve of me at all times, but I know it will never happen. So instead of striving incessantly for their approval, I can toughen myself up so I can stand their disapproval more easily. When I get to the point where disapproval leaves me mildly uncomfortable rather than upset, I have taken 10 giant steps toward happiness!

Life Should Be Fair

It isn't. Perhaps parents do children a disservice by preaching fairness so much. Kids need to learn life is *not* fair. Sometimes life is unfair to our benefit. Occasionally when I'm grocery shopping, I find all the checkout counters stacked with shoppers waiting with loaded baskets. Just as I mosey up with my shopping cart, a clerk unfastens her chain and says, "I'll take you over here, Ma'am."

Is that fair? No way. Do I complain? Wouldn't think of it! That's just "good luck."

Do I wail, "Life is unfair," when I zip all the way downtown hitting green lights at every intersection? No, I just think, "Wow. Neat."

I save the "unfair" routine for the times I hit the red lights or someone else gets the newly opened checkout stand. I am convinced life is *not* fair, and it treats us all alike—unfairly. So what else is new? All we need to do is accept that fact, and we can take unfairness in our stride.

The next time your child comes home from school complaining, "Teacher made us all stay in during recess just 'cause two kids were talking! That's not fair!" you can say pleasantly, "No, it isn't, is it? Lots of things in life are not fair."

Sometimes, when I feel unfairly treated, I like to make a mental list of some more unfairnesses I'm aware of. How come *I* have four beautiful children, when some people don't? Why do *I* deserve such good health, when some friends have all kinds of ailments? How is it *I* get to live in a nice house, when some people have to live in slums? And so on. Life *is* unfair, but a lot of times it works to our benefit.

A Last Look at Apples

Lisa recently discovered McIntosh apples and has pronounced them the best eating in the world. Larry and Lindsay like crisp, red delicious apples. Lyle prefers tart, golden ones. Laurie loves a juicy winesap. I love hard, sour pippins. Fortunately all these different kinds of apples are available in the market at certain times of the year. We can indulge ourselves and feel good about it because everyone knows how healthy we become if we eat apples every day!

So much for real apples. The other kind, the ones this book is about, may not be plentiful, but they're every bit as important as real apples. We might call them *emotional apples*. When I keep my barrel filled to the brim with luscious emotional apples, I'm able to be my very happiest and always have plenty to give to the people around me.

Sometimes my barrel gets emptied before I know it. It isn't until I realize I've snapped at everyone in the house during the past few hours that I become aware I'm out of apples. Awareness is the first step. Once I know I'm empty, it's just a matter of replenishing them and all is well again.

I always get to decide what kind of apples I want. There are so many varieties. What I want today might be very different from what I wanted yesterday.

When I've been busy rushing wild-eyed from place to place, and I feel fragmented and overextended, the best apple for me might be total aloneness. I want to be quiet and not have to say a word to anyone. I might just sit and look out the window.

Other times I might want to be quiet but doing something productive. Being creative gives me a lot of apples, so I might cut out a dress to sew, make a carrot cake or write a letter. I'd want to do it all by myself, with no need for conversation.

Then there are times I want intimacy. I want to be alone with Larry for a relaxing conversation about the day. Sharing works best for me when it's between just two people, whether it's laughing with Laurie, having lunch with Lisa, soul-searching with Lindsay or buying carpeting with Lyle.

It's important to realize what we want at the moment. If I've talked all day to clients or classes, giving a party is more of the same and might be more tiring than enjoyable. On the other hand, if I've spent the day alone with housekeeping, a party might be just the ticket. To surround myself with people and talk and laugh a lot is energizing and creates the perfect balance in my day.

It's fun to think about the possibilities open to us and know apples are there just for the taking. If I find myself alone and lonely, I hope I realize I need people. I can set about finding some by phone or by a visit. The important thing is knowing *I have the responsibility for getting whatever apples I want!* If I don't take that responsibility, it's my own fault. I can't blame anyone else if I'm bored, overworked or unhappy.

Once I figure out what kinds of apples I like best, it helps to tell the people closest to me about them and invite them to tell me about their apple tastes. We can be almost sure to differ. I love to dance, so going dancing is an apple-filled experience for me. The only trouble is I need a partner to dance with, and Larry is not eager to dance. He prefers going to a movie. We just agree to give each other apples. I give him one by going to the movie, and he gives me one by going dancing afterward. Both of us win. But we have to share our feelings and desires to negotiate the trade.

It's marvelous we never need to worry about running out of apples and being unable to get more. We can feel perfectly free to give them away by the dozen to lots of people. There's an endless supply from which to replenish them. There are millions of ways to get apples. Many ways we haven't even thought of yet. The only danger is not making the effort to get them.

There are three life tasks to which we need to apply ourselves if we want to be fully happy—work, friendship and love. All of them take apples. And all of them *give* apples. Giving or taking, apples make life worth living!

It might be fun for you and the "significant other" person in your life to make and exchange lists of apples. In making a list, we stretch our thinking a bit and frequently come up with some new ideas.

Once you have your list, on paper or in your head, use it! Keep your barrel full to overflowing. Give apples freely from it because that's a source of apples in itself. It's fun to give.

Additional References

Bisch, Louis E. *Be Glad You're Neurotic.* New York: McGraw-Hill Paperbacks, 1974.

Dewey, Edith. *Basic Applications of Adlerian Psychology.* Coral Springs, FL: CMTI Press, 1981.

Ellis, Albert and Robert A. Harper. *A New Guide to Rational Living.* Hollywood, CA: Wilshire Books, 1975.

Ellis, Albert and Irving Becker. *A Guide to Personal Happiness.* Hollywood, CA: Wilshire Books, 1982.

Dreikurs, R. and V. Soltz. *Children: the Challenge.* New York: Hawthorne Books, Inc., 1964.

Harris, Thomas. *I'm OK, You're OK.* New York: Harper and Row, 1967.

Kennedy, Eugene. *If You Really Knew Me Would You Still Like Me?* Allen, TX: Argus Communications, 1975.

Kern, Roy. *Lifestyle Priorities.* Coral Springs, FL: CMTI Press, 1982.

Powell, John, S.J. *Why Am I Afraid To Tell You Who I Am?* Allen, TX: Argus Communications, 1969.

Index